Social Rights and Duties - Volume I

LESLIE STEPHEN

Published in 1896

TABLE OF CONTENTS

NOTE

The following chapters are chiefly a republication of addresses delivered to the Ethical Societies of London. Some have previously appeared in the International Journal of Ethics, the National Review, and the Contemporary Review. The author has to thank the proprietors of these periodicals for their consent to the republication.
L. S.

THE AIMS OF ETHICAL SOCIETIES

I am about to say a few words upon the aims of this society: and I should be sorry either to exaggerate or to depreciate our legitimate pretensions. It would be altogether impossible to speak too strongly of the importance of the great questions in which our membership of the society shows us to be interested. It would, I fear, be easy enough to make an over-estimate of the part which we can expect to play in their solution. I hold indeed, or I should not be here, that we may be of some service at any rate to each other. I think that anything which stimulates an active interest in the vital problems of the day deserves the support of all thinking men; and I propose to consider briefly some of the principles by which we should be guided in doing whatever we can to promote such an interest.

We are told often enough that we are living in a period of important intellectual and social revolutions. In one way we are perhaps inclined even to state the fact a little too strongly. We suffer at times from the common illusion that the problems of to-day are entirely new: we fancy that nobody ever thought of them before, and that when we have solved them, nobody will ever need to look for another solution. To ardent reformers in all ages it seems as if the millennium must begin with their triumph, and that their triumph will be established by a single victory. And while some of us are thus sanguine, there are many who see in the struggles of to-day the approach of a deluge which is to sweep away all that once ennobled life. The believer in the old creeds, who fears that faith is decaying, and the supernatural life fading from the world, denounces the modern spirit as materialising and degrading. The conscience of mankind, he thinks, has become drugged and lethargic; our minds are fixed upon sensual pleasures, and our conduct regulated by a blind struggle for the maximum of luxurious enjoyment. The period in his eyes is a period of growing corruption; modern society suffers under a complication of mortal diseases, so widely spread and deeply seated that at present there is no hope of regeneration. The best hope is that its decay may provide the soil in which seed may be sown of a far-distant growth of happier augury. Such dismal forebodings are no novelty. Every age produces its prophecies of coming woes. Nothing would be easier than to make out a catena of testimonies from great men at every stage of the world's history, declaring each in turn that the cup of iniquity was now at last overflowing, and that corruption had reached so unprecedented a step that some great catastrophe must be approaching. A man of unusually lofty morality is, for that reason, more keenly sensitive to the lowness of the average standard, and too easily accepts the belief that the evils before his eyes must be in fact greater, and not, as may perhaps be the case, only more vividly perceived, than those of the bygone ages. A call to repentance easily takes the form of an assertion that the devil is getting the upper hand; and we may hope that the pessimist view is only a form of the discontent which is a necessary condition of improvement. Anyhow, the diametrical conflict of prophecies suggests one remark which often impresses me. We are bound to call each other by terribly hard names. A gentleman assures me in print that I am playing the devil's game; depriving my victims, if I have any, of all the beliefs that can make life noble or happy, and doing my best to destroy the very first principles of morality. Yet I meet my adversary in the flesh, and find that he treats me not only with courtesy, but with no inconsiderable amount of sympathy. He admits-by his actions and his argument-that I-the miserable sophist and seducer-have not only some good impulses, but have really something to say which deserves a careful and respectful answer. An infidel, a century or two ago, was supposed to have forfeited all claim to the ordinary decencies of life. Now I can say, and can say with real satisfaction, that I do not find any difference of creed, however vast in words, to be an obstacle to decent and even friendly treatment. I am at times tempted to ask whether my opponent can be quite logical in being so courteous; whether, if he is as sure as he says that I am in the devil's service, I ought not, as a matter of duty, to be encountered with the old dogmatism and arrogance. I shall, however, leave my friends of a different way of thinking to settle that point for themselves. I cannot doubt the sincerity of their courtesy, and I will hope that it is somehow consistent with their logic. Rather I will try to meet them in a corresponding spirit by a brief confession. I have often enough spoken too harshly and vehemently of my antagonists. I have tried to fix upon them too unreservedly what seemed to me the logical consequences of their dogmas. I have condemned their attempts at a milder interpretation of their creed as proofs of insincerity, when I ought to have done more justice to the legitimate and lofty motives which prompted them. And I at least am bound by my own views to admit that even the antagonist from whose utterances I differ most widely may be an unconscious ally, supplementing rather than contradicting my theories, and in great part moved by aspirations which I ought to recognise even when allied with what I take to be defective reasoning. We are all amenable to one great influence. The vast shuttle of modern life is weaving together all races and creeds and classes. We are no longer shut up in separate compartments, where the mental horizon is limited by the area visible from the parish steeple; each little section can no longer fancy, in the old childish fashion, that its own arbitrary prejudices and dogmas are parts of the eternal order of things; or infer that in the indefinite region beyond, there live nothing but monsters and anthropophagi, and men whose heads grow beneath their shoulders. The annihilation of space has made us fellows as by a kind of mechanical compulsion; and every advance of knowledge has increased the impossibility of taking our little church-little in comparison with mankind, be it even as great as the Catholic Church-for the one pattern of right belief. The first effect of bringing remote nations and classes into closer contact is often an explosion of antipathy; but in the long run it means a development of human sympathy. Wide, therefore, as is the opposition of opinions as to what is the true theory of the world-as to which is the divine and which the diabolical element-I fully believe that beneath the war of words and dogmas there is a growth of genuine toleration, and, we must hope, of ultimate conciliation.

This is manifest in another direction. The churches are rapidly making at least one discovery. They are beginning to find out that their vitality depends not upon success in theological controversy, but upon their success in meeting certain social needs and aspirations common to all classes. It is simply impossible for any thinking man at the present day to take any living interest, for example, in the ancient controversies. The "drum ecclesiastic" of the seventeenth century would sound a mere lullaby to us. Here and there a priest or a belated dissenting minister may amuse himself by threshing out once more the old chaff of dead and buried dogmas. There are people who can argue gravely about baptismal regeneration or apostolical succession. Such doctrines were once alive, no doubt, because they represented the form in which certain still living problems had then to present themselves. They now require to be stated in a totally different shape, before we can even guess why they were once so exciting, or how men could have supposed their modes of attacking the question to be adequate. The Pope and General Booth still condemn each other's tenets; and in case of need would, I suppose, take down the old rusty weapons from the armoury. But each sees with equal clearness that the real stress of battle lies elsewhere. Each tries, after his own fashion, to give a better answer than the Socialists to the critical problems of to-day. We ought so far to congratulate both them and ourselves on the direction of their energies. Nay, can we not even co-operate, and put these hopeless controversies aside? Why not agree to differ about the questions which no one denies to be all but insoluble, and become allies in promoting morality? Enormous social forces find their natural channel through the churches; and if the beliefs inculcated by the church were not, as believers assert, the ultimate cause of progress, it is at least clear that they were not incompatible with progress. The church, we all now admit, whether by reason of or in spite of its dogmatic creed, was for ages one great organ of civilisation, and still exercises an incalculable influence. Why, then, should we, who cannot believe in the dogmas, yet fall into line with believers for practical purposes? Churches insist verbally upon the importance of their dogma: they are bound to do so by their logical position; but, in reality, for them, as for us, the dogma has become in many ways a mere excrescence-a survival of barren formulæ which do little harm to anybody. Carlyle, in his quaint phrase, talked about the exodus from Houndsditch, but doubted whether it were yet time to cast aside the Hebrew old clothes. They have become threadbare and antiquated. That gives a reason to the intelligent for abandoning them; but, also, perhaps a reason for not quarrelling with those who still care to masquerade in them. Orthodox people have made a demand that the Board Schools should teach certain ancient doctrines about the nature of Christ; and the demand strikes some of us as preposterous if not hypocritical. But putting aside the audacity of asking unbelievers to pay for such teaching, one might be tempted to ask, what harm could it really do? Do you fancy for a moment that you can really teach a child of ten the true meaning of the Incarnation? Can you give him more than a string of words as meaningless as magical formulæ? I was brought up at the most orthodox of Anglican seminaries. I learned the Catechism, and heard lectures upon the Thirty-nine Articles. I never found that the teaching had ever any particular effect upon my mind. As I grew up, the obsolete exuviæ of doctrine dropped off my mind like dead leaves from a tree. They could not get any vital hold in an atmosphere of tolerable enlightenment. Why should we fear the attempt to instil these fragments of decayed formulæ into the minds of children of tender age? Might we not be certain that they would vanish of themselves? They are superfluous, no doubt, but too futile to be of any lasting importance. I remember that, when the first Education Act was being discussed, mention was made of a certain Jew who not only sent his son to a Christian school, but insisted upon his attending all the lessons. He had paid his fees, he said, for education in the Gospels among other things, and he meant to have his money's worth. "But your son," it was urged, "will become a Christian." "I," he replied, "will take good care of that at home." Was not the Jew a man of sense? Can we suppose that the mechanical repetition of a few barren phrases will do either harm or good? As the child develops he will, we may hope, remember his multiplication table, and forget his fragments of the Athanasian Creed. Let the wheat and tares be planted together, and trust to the superior vitality of the more valuable plant. The sentiment might be expressed sentimentally as easily as cynically. We may urge, like many sceptics of the last century, that Christianity should be kept "for the use of the poor," and renounced in the esoteric creed of the educated. Or we may urge the literary and æsthetic beauty of the old training, and wish it to be preserved to discipline the imagination, though we may reject its value as a historical statement of fact.

The audience which I am addressing has, I presume, made up its mind upon such views. They come too late. It might have been a good thing, had it been possible, to effect the transition from old to new without a violent convulsion: good, if Christian conceptions had been slowly developed into more simple forms; if the beautiful symbols had been retained till they could be impregnated with a new meaning; and if the new teaching of science and philosophy had gradually percolated into the ancient formulæ without causing a disruption. Possibly the Protestant Reformation was a misfortune, and Erasmus saw the truth more clearly than Luther. I cannot go into might-have-beens. We have to deal with facts. A conspiracy of silence is impossible about matters which have been vehemently discussed for centuries. We have to take sides; and we at least have agreed to take the side of the downright thinker, who will say nothing that he does not believe, and hide nothing that he does believe, and speak out his mind without reservation or economy and accommodation. Indeed, as things are, any other course seems to me to be impossible. I have spoken, for example, of General Booth. Many people heartily admire his schemes of social reform, and have been willing to subscribe for its support, without troubling themselves about his theology. I will make no objection; but I confess that I could not therefore treat that theology as either morally or intellectually respectable. It has happened to me once or twice to listen to expositions from orators of the Salvation Army. Some of them struck me as sincere though limited, and others as the victims of an overweening vanity. The oratory, so far as I could hear, consisted in stringing together an endless set of phrases about the blood of Christ, which, if they really meant anything, meant a doctrine as low in the intellectual scale as that of any of the objects of missionary enterprise. The conception of the transactions between God and man was apparently modelled upon the dealings of a petty tradesman. The "blood of Christ" was regarded like the panacea of a quack doctor, which will cure the sins of anybody who accepts the prescription. For anything I can say, such a creed may be elevating-relatively: elevating as slavery is said to have been elevating when it was a substitute for extermination. The hymns of the Army may be better than public-house melodies, and the excitement produced less mischievous than that due to gin. But the best that I can wish for its adherents is, that they should speedily reach a point at which they could perceive their doctrines to be debasing. I hope, indeed, that they do not realise their own meaning: but I could almost as soon join in some old pagan ceremonies, gash my body with knives, or swing myself from a hook, as indulge in this variety of spiritual intoxication.

There are, it is true, plenty of more refined and intellectual preachers, whose sentiments deserve at least the respect due to tender and humane feeling. They have found a solution, satisfactory to themselves, of the great dilemma which presses on so many minds. A religion really to affect the vulgar must be a superstition; to satisfy the thoughtful, it must be a philosophy. Is it possible to contrive so to fuse the crude with the refined as to make at least a working compromise? To me personally, and to most of us living at the present day, the enterprise appears to be impracticable. My own experience is, I imagine, a very common one. When I ceased to accept the teaching of my youth, it was not so much a process of giving up beliefs, as of discovering that I had never really believed. The contrast between the genuine convictions which guide and govern our conduct, and the professions which we were taught to repeat in church, when once realised, was too glaring. One belonged to the world of realities, and the other to the world of dreams. The orthodox formulæ represent, no doubt, a sentiment, an attempt to symbolise emotions which might be beautiful, or to indicate vague impressions about the tendency of things in general; but to put them side by side with real beliefs about facts was to reveal their flimsiness. The "I believe" of the creed seemed to mean something quite different from the "I believe" of politics and history and science. Later experience has only deepened and strengthened that feeling. Kind and loving and noble-minded people have sought to press upon me the consolations of their religion. I thank them in all sincerity; and I feel,-why should I not admit it?-that it may be a genuine comfort to set your melancholy to the old strain in which so many generations have embodied their sorrows and their aspirations. And yet to me, its consolation is an invitation to reject plain facts; to seek for refuge in a shadowy world of dreams and conjectures, which dissolve as you try to grasp them. The doctrine offered for my acceptance cannot be stated without qualifications and reserves and modifications, which make it as useless as it is vague and conjectural. I may learn in time to submit to the inevitable; I cannot drug myself with phrases which evaporate as soon as they are exposed to a serious test. You profess to give me the only motives of conduct; and I know that at the first demand to define them honestly-to say precisely what you believe and why you believe it-you will be forced to withdraw, and explain and evade, and at last retire to the safe refuge of a mystery, which might as well be admitted at starting. As I have read and thought, I have been more and more impressed with the obvious explanation of these observations. How should the beliefs be otherwise than shadowy and illusory, when their very substance is made of doubts laboriously and ingeniously twisted into the semblance of convictions? In one way or other that is the characteristic mark of the theological systems of the present day. Proof is abandoned for persuasion. The orthodox believer professed once to prove the facts which he asserted and to show that his dogmas expressed the truth. He now only tries to show that the alleged facts don't matter, and that the dogmas are meaningless. Nearly two centuries ago, for example, a deist pointed out that the writer of the Book of Daniel, like other people, must have written after the events which he mentioned. All the learned, down to Dr. Pusey, denounced his theory, and declared his argument to be utterly destructive of the faith. Now an orthodox professor will admit that the deist was perfectly right, and only tries to persuade himself that arguments from facts are superfluous. The supposed foundation is gone: the superstructure is not to be affected. What the keenest disputant now seeks to show is, not that the truth of the records can be established beyond reasonable doubt; but that no absolute contradiction in terms is involved in supposing that they correspond more or less roughly to something which may possibly have happened. So long as a thing is not proved false by mathematical demonstration, I may still continue to take it for a divine revelation, and to listen respectfully when experienced statesmen and learned professors assure me with perfect gravity that they can believe in Noah's flood or in the swine of Gadara. They have an unquestionable right to believe if they please: and they expect me to accept the facts for the sake of the doctrine. There, unluckily, I have a similar difficulty. It is the orthodox who are the systematic sceptics. The most famous philosophers of my youth endeavoured to upset the deist by laying the foundation of Agnosticism, arbitrarily tagged to an orthodox conclusion. They told me to believe a doctrine because it was totally impossible that I should know whether it was true or not, or indeed attach any real meaning to it whatever. The highest altar, as Sir W. Hamilton said, was the altar to the unknown and unknowable God. Others, seeing the inevitable tendency of such methods, have done their best to find in that the Christian doctrine, rightly understood, the embodiment of the highest philosophy. It is the divine voice which speaks in our hearts, though it has caught some accretion of human passion and superstition. The popular versions are false and debased; the old versions of the Atonement, for example, monstrous; and the belief in the everlasting torture of sinners, a hideous and groundless caricature. With much that such men have said I could, of course, agree heartily; for, indeed, it expresses the strongest feelings which have caused religious revolt. But would it not be simpler to say, "the doctrine is not true," than to say, "it is true, but means just the reverse of what it was also taken to mean"? I prefer plain terms; and "without doubt he shall perish everlastingly" seems to be an awkward way of denying the endlessness of punishment. You cannot denounce the immorality of the old dogmas with the infidel, and then proclaim their infinite value with the believer. You defend the doctrine by showing that in its plain downright sense,-the sense in which it embodied popular imaginations,-it was false and shocking. The proposal to hold by the words evacuated of the old meaning is a concession of the whole case to the unbeliever, and a substitution of sentiment and aspiration for a genuine intellectual belief. Explaining away, however dexterously and delicately, is not defending, but at once confessing error, and encumbering yourself with all the trammels of misleading associations. The more popular method, therefore, at the present day is not to rationalise, but to try to outsceptic the sceptic. We are told that we have no solid ground from reason at all, and that even physical science is as full of contradictions as theology. Such enterprises, conducted with whatever ingenuity, are, as I believe, hopeless; but at least they are fundamentally and radically sceptical. That, under whatever disguises, is the true meaning of the Catholic argument, which is so persuasive to many. To prove the truth of Christianity by abstract reasoning may be hopeless; but nothing is easier than to persuade yourself to believe it, if once you will trust instinct in place of reason, and forget that instinct proves anything and everything. The success of such arguments with thoughtful men is simply a measure of the spread of scepticism. The conviction that truth is unattainable is the master argument for submitting to "authority". The "authority," in the scientific sense of any set of men who agree upon a doctrine, varies directly as their independence of each other. Their "authority" in the legal sense varies as the closeness of their mutual dependence. As the consent loses its value logically, it gains in power of coercion. And therefore it is easy to substitute drilling for arguing, and to take up a belief as you accept admission to a society, as a matter of taste and feeling, with which abstract logic has nothing to do. The common dilemma-you must be a Catholic or an atheist-means, that theology is only tenable if you drill people into belief by a vast organisation appealing to other than logical motives.

I do not argue these points: I only indicate what I take to be your own conviction as well as mine. It seems to me, in fact, that the present state of mind-if we look to men's real thoughts and actions, not to their conventional phrases-is easily definable. It is simply a tacit recognition that the old orthodoxy cannot be maintained either by the evidence of facts or by philosophical argument. It has puzzled me sometimes to understand why the churches should insist upon nailing themselves down to the truth of their dogmas and their legendary history. Why cannot they say frankly, what they seem to be constantly on the verge of saying-Our dogmas and our history are not true, or not "true" in the historical or scientific sense of the word? To ask for such truth in the sphere of theology is as pedantic as to ask for it in the sphere of poetry. Poetical truth means, not that certain events actually happened, or that the poetical "machinery" is to be taken as an existing fact; but that the poem is, so to speak, the projection of truths upon the cloudland of imagination. It reflects and gives sensuous images of truth; but it is only the Philistine or the blockhead who can seriously ask, is it true? Some such position seems to be really conceivable as an ultimate compromise. Put aside the prosaic insistence upon literal matter-of-fact truth, and we may all agree to use the same symbolism, and interpret it as we please. This seems to me to be actually the view of many thoughtful people, though for obvious reasons it is not often explicitly stated. One reason is, of course, the consciousness that the great mass of mankind requires plain, tangible motives for governing its life; and if it once be admitted that so much of the orthodox doctrine is mere symbolism or adumbration of truths, the admission would involve the loss of the truths so indicated. Moral conduct, again, and moral beliefs are supposed to depend upon some affirmation of these truths; and excellent people are naturally shy of any open admission which may appear to throw doubt upon the ultimate grounds of morality.

Indeed, if it could be really proved that men have to choose between renouncing moral truths and accepting unproved theories, it might be right- I will not argue the point-to commit intellectual suicide. If the truth is that we are mere animals or mere automata, shall we sacrifice the truth, or sacrifice what we have at least agreed to call our higher nature? For us the dilemma has no force: for we do not admit the discrepancy. We believe that morality depends upon something deeper and more permanent than any of the dogmas that have hitherto been current in the churches. It is a product of human nature, not of any of these transcendental speculations or faint survivals of traditional superstitions. Morality has grown up independently of, and often in spite of, theology. The creeds have been good so far as they have accepted or reflected the moral convictions; but it is an illusion to suppose that they have generated it. They represent the dialect and the imagery by which moral truths have been conveyed to minds at certain stages of thought; but it is a complete inversion of the truth to suppose that the morality sprang out of them. From this point of view we must of necessity treat the great ethical questions independently. We cannot form a real alliance with thinkers radically opposed to us. Divines tell us that we reject the one possible basis of morality. To us it appears that we are strengthening it, by severing it from a connection with doctrines arbitrary, incapable of proof, and incapable of retaining any consistent meaning. Theologians once believed that hell-fire was the ultimate sentence, and persecution the absolute duty of every Christian ruler. The churches which once burnt and exterminated are now only anxious to proclaim freedom of belief, and to cast the blame of persecution upon their rivals. Divines have discovered that the doctrine of hell-fire deserves all that infidels have said of it; and a member of Dante's church was arguing the other day that hell might on the whole be a rather pleasant place of residence. Doctrines which can thus be turned inside out are hardly desirable bases for morality. So the early Christians, again, were the Socialists of their age, and took a view of Dives and Lazarus which would commend itself to the Nihilists of to-day. The church is now often held up to us as the great barrier against Socialism, and the one refuge against subversive doctrines. In a well-known essay on "People whom one would have wished to have seen," Lamb and his friends are represented as agreeing that if Christ were to enter they would all fall down and worship Him. It may have been so; but if the man who best represents the ideas of early Christians were to enter a respectable society of to-day, would it not be more likely to send for the police? When we consider such changes, and mark in another direction how the dogmas which once set half the world to cut the throats of the other half, have sunk into mere combinations of hard words, can we seriously look to the maintenance of dogmas, even in the teeth of reason, as a guarantee for ethical convictions? What you call retaining the only base of morality, appears to us to be trying to associate morality with dogmas essentially arbitrary and unreasonable.

From this point of view it is naturally our opinion that we should promote all thorough discussion of great ethical problems in a spirit and by methods which are independent of the orthodox dogmas. There are many such problems undoubtedly of the highest importance. The root of all the great social questions of which I have spoken lies in the region of Ethics; and upon that point, at least, we can go along with much that is said upon the orthodox side. We cannot, indeed, agree that Ethics can be adequately treated by men pledged to ancient traditions, employing antiquated methods, and always tempted to have an eye to the interest of their own creeds and churches. But we can fully agree that ethical principles underlie all the most important problems. Every great religious reform has been stimulated by the conviction that the one essential thing is a change of spirit, not a mere modification of the external law, which has ceased to correspond to genuine beliefs and powerful motives. The commonest criticism, indeed, of all projectors of new Utopias is that they propose a change of human nature. The criticism really suggests a sound criterion. Unless the change proposed be practicable, the Utopia will doubtless be impossible. And unless some practicable change be proposed, the Utopia, even were it embodied in practice, would be useless. If the sole result of raising wages were an increase in the consumption of gin, wages might as well stay at a minimum. But the tacit assumption that all changes of human nature are impracticable is simply a cynical and unproved assertion. All of us here hold, I imagine, that human nature has in a sense been changed. We hold that, with all its drawbacks, progress is not an illusion; that men have become at least more tolerant and more humane; that ancient brutalities have become impossible; and that the suffering of the weaker excites a keener sympathy. To say that, in that sense, human nature must be changed, is to say only that the one sound criterion of all schemes for social improvement lies in their ethical tendency. The standard of life cannot be permanently raised unless you can raise the standard of motive. Old-fashioned political theorists thought that a simple change of the constitutional machinery would of itself remedy all evils, and failed to recognise that behind the institutions lie all the instincts and capabilities of the men who are to work them. A similar fallacy is prevalent, I fancy, in regard to what we call social reforms. Some scheme for a new mode of distributing the products of industry would, it is often assumed, remedy all social evils. To my thinking, no such change would do more than touch the superficial evils, unless it had also some tendency to call out the higher and repress the lower impulses. Unless we can to some extent change "human nature," we shall be weaving ropes of sand, or devising schemes for perpetual motion, for driving our machinery more effectively without applying fresh energy. We shall be falling into the old blunders; approving Jack Cade's proposal-as recorded by Shakespeare-that the three-hooped pot should have seven hoops; or attempting to get rid of poverty by converting the whole nation into paupers. No one, perhaps, will deny this in terms; and to admit it frankly is to admit that every scheme must be judged by its tendency to "raise the manhood of the poor," and to make every man, rich and poor, feel that he is discharging a useful function in society. Old Robert Owen, when he began his reforms, rested his doctrine and his hopes of perfectibility upon the scientific application of a scheme for "the formation of character". His plans were crude enough, and fell short of success. But he had seen the real conditions of success; and when, in after years, he imagined that a new society might be made by simply collecting men of any character in a crowd, and inviting them to share alike, he fell into the inevitable failure. Modern Socialists might do well to remember his history.

Now it is, as I understand, primarily the aim of an Ethical Society to promote the rational discussion of these underlying ethical principles. We wish to contribute to the clearest understanding we can of the right ends to which human energy should be devoted, and of the conditions under which such devotion is most likely to be rewarded with success. We desire to see the great controversy carried on in the nearest possible approach to a scientific spirit. That phrase implies, as I have said, that we must abandon much of the old guidance. The lights by which our ancestors professed to direct their course are not for us supernatural signs, shining in a transcendental region, but at most the beacons which they had themselves erected, and valuable as indications, though certainly not as infallible guides, to the right path. We must question everything, and be prepared to modify or abandon whatever is untenable. We must be scientific in spirit, in so far as we must trust nothing but a thorough and systematic investigation of facts, however the facts may be interpreted. Undoubtedly, the course marked out is long and arduous. It is perfectly true, moreover, as our antagonists will hasten to observe, that professedly scientific reasoners are hardly better agreed than their opponents. If they join upon some negative conclusions, and upon some general principles of method, they certainly do not reach the same results. They have at present no definite creed to lay down. I need only refer, for example, to one very obvious illustration. The men who were most conspicuous for their attempt to solve social problems by scientific methods, and most confident that they had succeeded, were, probably, those who founded the so-called "classical" political economy, and represented what is now called the individualist point of view. Government, they were apt to think, should do nothing but stand aside, see fair-play, and keep our knives from each other's throats and our hands out of each other's pockets. Much as their doctrines were denounced, this view is still represented by the most popular philosopher of the day. And undoubtedly we shall do well to take to heart the obvious moral. If we still believe in the old-fashioned doctrines, we must infer that to work out a scientific doctrine is by no means to secure its acceptance. If we reject them we must argue that the mere claim to be scientific may inspire men with a premature self-confidence, which tends only to make their errors more systematic. When, however, I look at the actual course of controversy, I am more impressed by another fact. "Individualism" is sometimes met by genuine argument. More frequently, I think, it is met by simple appeal to sentiment. This kind of thing, we are told, is exploded; it is not up to date; it is as obsolete as the plesiosaurus; and therefore, without bothering ourselves about your reasoning, we shall simply neglect it. Talk as much as you please, we can get a majority on the other side. We shall disregard your arguments, and, therefore-it is a common piece of logic at the present day-your arguments must be all wrong. I must be content here with simply indicating my own view. I think, in fact, that, in this as in other cases, the true answer to extreme theorists would be very different. I hold that we would begin by admitting the immense value of the lesson taught by the old individualists, if that be their right name. If they were precipitate in laying down "iron laws" and proclaiming inexorable necessity, they were perfectly right in pointing out that there are certain "laws of human nature," and conditions of social welfare, which will not be altered by simply declaring them to be unpleasant. They did an inestimable service in emphatically protesting against the system of forcibly suppressing, or trying to suppress, deep-seated evils, without an accurate preliminary diagnosis of the causes. And-not to go into remote questions-the "individualist" creed had this merit, which is related to our especial aims. The ethical doctrine which they preached may have had-I think that it had-many grave defects; but at least it involved a recognition of the truth which their opponents are too apt to shun or reject. They, at least, asserted strenuously the cardinal doctrine of the importance of individual responsibility. They might draw some erroneous inferences, but they could not put too emphatically the doctrine that men must not be taught to shift the blame of all their sufferings upon some mysterious entity called society, or expect improvement unless, among other virtues, they will cultivate the virtue of strenuous, unremitting, masculine self-help.

If this be at all true, it may indicate what I take to be the aim of our society, or rather of us as members of an ethical society. We hold, that is, that the great problems of to-day have their root, so to speak, in an ethical soil. They will be decided one way or other by the view which we take of ethical questions. The questions, for example, of what is meant by social justice, what is the justification of private property, or the limits of personal liberty, all lead us ultimately to ethical foundations. The same is, of course, true of many other problems. The demand for political rights of women is discussed, rightly no doubt, upon grounds of justice, and takes us to some knotty points. Does justice imply the equality of the sexes; and, if so, in what sense of "equality"? And, beyond this, we come to the question, What would be the bearing of our principles upon the institution of marriage, and upon the family bond? No question can be more important, or more vitally connected with Ethics. We, at any rate, can no longer answer such problems by any traditional dogmatism. They-and many other questions which I need not specify-have been asked, and have yet to be answered. They will probably not be answered by a simple yes or no, nor by any isolated solution of a metaphysical puzzle. Undoubtedly, a vast mass of people will insist upon being consulted, and will adopt methods which cannot be regarded as philosophical. Therefore, it is a matter of pressing importance that all people who can think at all should use their own minds, and should do their best to widen and strengthen the influence of the ablest thinkers. The chaotic condition of the average mind is our reason for trying to strengthen the influence, always too feeble, of the genuine thinkers. Much that passes itself off for thought is simply old prejudice in a new dress. Tradition has always this, indeed, to say for itself: that it represents the product of much unconscious reasoning from experience, and that it is at least compatible with such progress as has been hitherto achieved. Progress has in future to take place in the daylight, and under the stress of keen discussion from every possible point of view. It would be rash indeed to assume that we can hope to see the substitution of purely rational and scientific methods for the old haphazard and tentative blundering into slightly better things. It is possible enough that the creed of the future may, after all, be a compromise, admitting some elements of higher truth, but attracting the popular mind by concessions to superstition and ignorance. We can hardly hope to get rid of the rooted errors which have so astonishing a vitality. But we should desire, and, so far as in us lies, endeavour to secure the presence of the largest possible element of genuine and reasoned conviction in the faith of our own and the rising generation.

I have not sought to say anything new. I have only endeavoured to define the general position which we, as I imagine, have agreed to accept. We hold in common that the old dogmas are no longer tenable, though we are very far from being agreed as to what should replace them. We have each, I dare say, our own theory; we agree that our theories, whatever they may be, are in need of strict examination, of verification, it may be, but it may be also of modification or rejection. We hope that such societies as this may in the first place serve as centres for encouraging and popularising the full and free discussion of the great questions. We wish that people who have reached a certain stage of cultivation should be made aware of the course which is being taken by those who may rightly claim to be in the van. We often wish to know, as well as we can, what is the direction of the deeper currents of thought; what genuine results, for example, have been obtained by historical criticism, especially as applied to the religious history of the world; we want to know what are the real points now at issue in the world of science; the true bearing of the theories of evolution, and so forth, which are known by name far beyond the circle in which their logical reasoning is really appreciated; we want to know, again, what are the problems which really interest modern metaphysicians or psychologists; in what directions there seems to be a real promise of future achievement, and in what directions it seems to be proved by experience that any further expansion of intellectual energy is certain to result only in the discovery of mares' nests. Matthew Arnold would have expressed this by saying that we are required to be made accessible to the influence of the Zeitgeist. There is a difficulty, no doubt, in discovering by what signs we may recognise the utterances of the Zeitgeist; and distinguish between loyalty to the real intellectual leaders and a simple desire to be arrayed in the last new fashion in philosophy. There is no infallible sign; and, yet, a genuine desire to discover the true lines in which thought is developing, is not of the less importance. Arnold, like others, pointed the moral by a contrast between England and Germany. The best that has been done in England, it is said, has generally been done by amateurs and outsiders. They have, perhaps, certain advantages, as being less afraid to strike into original paths, and even the originality of ignorance is not always, though it may be in nine cases out of ten, a name for fresh blundering. But if sporadic English writers have now and then hit off valuable thoughts, there can be no doubt that we have had a heavy price to pay. The comparative absence of any class, devoted, like German professors, to a systematic and combined attempt to spread the borders of knowledge and speculation, has been an evil which is the more felt in proportion as specialisation of science and familiarity with previous achievements become more important. It would be very easy to give particular instances of our backwardness. How different would have been the course of English church history, said somebody, if Newman had only known German! He would have breathed a larger air, and might have desisted-I suppose that was the meaning-from the attempt to put life into certain dead bones. And with equal truth, it may be urged, how much better work might have been done by J. S. Mill if he had really read Kant! He might not have been converted, but he would have been saved from maintaining in their crude form, doctrines which undoubtedly require modification. Under his reign, English thought was constantly busied with false issues, simply from ignorance of the most effective criticism. It is needless to point out how much time is wasted in the defence of positions that have long been turned by the enemy from sheer want of acquaintance with the relevant evidence, or with the logic that has been revealed by the slow thrashing out of thorough controversy. It would be invidious perhaps to insist too much upon another obvious result: the ease with which a man endowed with a gift of popular rhetoric, and a facility for catching at the current phrases, can set up as a teacher, however palpable to the initiated may be his ignorance. Scientific thought has perhaps as much to fear from the false prophets who take its name as from the open enemies who try to stifle its voice. I would rather emphasise another point, perhaps less generally remarked. The study has its idols as well as its market-place. Certain weaknesses are developed in the academical atmosphere as well as in the arenas of public discussion. Freeman used to say that English historians had avoided certain errors into which German writers of far greater knowledge and more thorough scholarship had fallen, simply because points were missed by a professor in a German university which were plain to those who, like many Englishmen, had to take a part in actual political work. I think that this is not without a meaning for us. We have learnt, very properly, to respect German research and industry; and we are trying in various directions to imitate their example. Perhaps it would be as well to keep an eye upon some German weaknesses. A philosophy made for professors is apt to be a philosophy for pedants. A professor is bound to be omniscient; he has to have an answer to everything; he is tempted to construct systems which will pass muster in the lecture-room, and to despise the rest of their applicability to daily life. I confess myself to be old-fashioned enough to share some of the old English prejudices against those gigantic structures which have been thrown out by imposing philosophers, who evolved complete systems of metaphysics and logic and religion and politics and æsthetics out of their own consciousness. We have multiplied professors of late, and professors are bound to write books, and to magnify the value of their own studies. They must make a show of possessing an encyclopædic theory which will explain everything and take into account all previous theories. Sometimes, perhaps, they will lose themselves in endless subtleties and logomachies and construct cobwebs of the brain, predestined to the rubbish-heap of extinct philosophies. It is enough, however, to urge that a mere student may be the better for keeping in mind the necessity of keeping in mind real immediate human interests; as the sentimentalist has to be reminded of the importance of strictly logical considerations. And I think too that a very brief study of the most famous systems of old days will convince us that philosophers should be content with a more modest attitude than they have sometimes adopted; give up the pretensions to framing off-hand theories of things in general, and be content to puzzle out a few imperfect truths which may slowly work their way into the general structure of thought. I wish to speak humbly as befits one who cannot claim any particular authority for his opinion. But, in all humility, I suggest that if we can persuade men of reputation in the regions where subtle thought and accurate research are duly valued, we shall be doing good, not only to ourselves, but, if I may whisper it, to them. We value their attainments so highly that we desire their influence to spread beyond the narrow precinct of university lecture-rooms; and their thoughts be, at the same time, stimulated and vitalised by bringing them into closer contact with the problems which are daily forced upon us in the business of daily life. A divorce between the men of thought and the men of action is really bad for both. Whatever tends to break up the intellectual stupor of large classes, to rouse their minds, to increase their knowledge of the genuine work that is being done, to provide them even with more of such recreations as refine and invigorate, must have our sympathy, and will be useful both to those who confer and to those who receive instruction. So, after all, a philosopher can learn few things of more importance than the art of translating his doctrines into language intelligible and really instructive to the outside world. There was a period when real thinkers, as Locke and Berkeley and Butler and Hume, tried to express themselves as pithily and pointedly as possible. They were, say some of their critics, very shallow: they were over-anxious to suit the taste of wits and the town: and in too much fear of the charge of pedantry. Well, if some of our profounder thinkers would try for once to pack all that they really have to say as closely as they can, instead of trying to play every conceivable change upon every thought that occurs to them, I fancy that they would be surprised both at the narrowness of the space which they would occupy and the comparative greatness of the effect they would produce.

An ethical society should aim at supplying a meeting-place between the expert and specialist on one side, and, on the other, with the men who have to apply ideas to the complex concretes of political and social activity. How far we can succeed in furthering that aim I need not attempt to say. But I will conclude by reverting to some thoughts at which I hinted at starting. You may think that I have hardly spoken in a very sanguine or optimistic tone. I have certainly admitted the existence of enormous difficulties and the probabilities of very imperfect success. I cannot think that the promised land of which we are taking a Pisgah sight is so near or the view so satisfactory as might be wished. A mirage like that which attended our predecessors may still be exercising illusions for us; and I anticipate less an immediate fruition, than a beginning of another long cycle of wanderings through a desert, let us hope rather more fertile than that which we have passed. If this be something of a confession you may easily explain it by personal considerations. In an old controversy which I was reading the other day, one of the disputants observed that his adversary held that the world was going from bad to worse. "I do not wonder at the opinion," he remarks; "for I am every day more tempted to embrace it myself, since every day I am leaving youth further behind." I am old enough to feel the force of that remark. Without admitting senility, I have lived long enough, that is, to know well that for me the brighter happiness is a thing of the past; that I have to look back even to realise what it means; and to feel that a sadder colouring is conferred upon the internal world by the eye "which hath kept watch o'er man's mortality." I have watched the brilliant promise of many contemporaries eclipsed by premature death; and have too often had to apply Newton's remark, "If that man had lived, we might have known something". Lights which once cheered me have gone out, and are going out all too rapidly; and, to say nothing of individuals, I have also lived long enough to watch the decay of once flourishing beliefs. I can remember, only too vividly, the confident hope with which many young men, whom I regarded as the destined leaders of progress, affirmed that the doctrines which they advocated were going forth conquering and to conquer; and though I may still think that those doctrines had a permanent value, and were far from deserving the reproaches now often levelled at them, I must admit that we greatly exaggerated our omniscience. I am often tempted, I confess, to draw the rather melancholy moral that some of my younger friends may be destined to disillusionment, and may be driven some thirty years hence to admit that their present confidence was a little in excess.

I admit all this: but I do not admit that my view could sanction despondency. I can see perhaps ground for foreboding which I should once have rejected. I can realise more distinctly, not only the amount of misery in the world, but the amount of misdirected energy, the dulness of the average intellect, and the vast deadweight of superstition and dread of the light with which all improvement must have to reckon. And yet I also feel that, if a complacent optimism be impossible, the world was never so full of interest. When we complain of the stress and strain and over-excitement of modern society we indicate, I think, a real evil; but we also tacitly admit that no one has any excuse for being dull. In every direction there is abundant opportunity for brave and thoughtful men to find the fullest occupation for whatever energy they may possess. There is work to be found everywhere in this sense, and none but the most torpid can find an excuse for joining the spiritually unemployed. The fields, surely, are white for the harvest, though there are weeds enough to be extirpated, and hard enough furrows to be ploughed. We know what has been done in the field of physical science. It has made the world infinite. The days of the old pagan, "suckled in some creed outworn," are regretted in Wordsworth's sonnet; for the old pagan held to the poetical view that a star was the chariot of a deity. The poor deity, however, had, in fact, a duty as monotonous as that of a driver in the Underground Railway. To us a star is a signal of a new world; it suggests universe beyond universe; sinking into the infinite abysses of space; we see worlds forming or decaying and raising at every moment problems of a strange fascination. The prosaic truth is really more poetical than the old figment of the childish imagination. The first great discovery of the real nature of the stars did, in fact, logically or not, break up more effectually than perhaps any other cause, the old narrow and stifling conception of the universe represented by Dante's superlative power; and made incredible the systems based on the conception that man can be the centre of all things and the universe created for the sake of this place. It is enough to point to the similar change due to modern theories of evolution. The impassable barriers of thought are broken down. Instead of the verbal explanation, which made every plant and animal an ultimate and inexplicable fact, we now see in each a movement in an indefinite series of complex processes, stretching back further than the eye can reach into the indefinite past. If we are sometimes stunned by the sense of inconceivable vastness, we feel, at least, that no intellectual conqueror need ever be affected by the old fear. For him there will always be fresh regions to conquer. Every discovery suggests new problems; and though knowledge may be simplified and codified, it will always supply a base for fresh explanations of the indefinite regions beyond. Can that which is true of the physical sciences be applied in any degree to the so-called moral sciences? To Bentham, I believe, is ascribed the wish that he could fall asleep and be waked at the end of successive centuries, to take note of the victories achieved in the intervals by his utilitarianism. Tennyson, in one of his youthful poems, played with the same thought. It would be pleasant, as the story of the sleeping beauty suggested, to rise every hundred years to mark the progress made in science and politics; and to see the "Titanic forces" that would come to the birth in divers climes and seasons; for we, he says-

For we are Ancients of the earth,

And in the morning of the times.

Tennyson, if this expressed his serious belief, seems to have lost his illusions; and it is probable enough that Bentham's would have had some unpleasant surprises could his wish have been granted. It is more than a century since his doctrine was first revealed, and yet the world has not become converted; and some people doubt whether it ever will be. If, indeed, Bentham's speculations had been adopted; if we had all become convinced that morality means aiming at the greatest happiness of the greatest number; if we were agreed as to what is happiness, and what is the best way of promoting it,-there would still have been a vast step to take, no less than to persuade people to desire to follow the lines of conduct which tend to minimise unhappiness. The mere intellectual conviction that this or that will be useful is quite a different thing from the desire. You no more teach men to be moral by giving them a sound ethical theory, than you teach them to be good shots by explaining the theory of projectiles. A religion implies a philosophy, but a philosophy is not by itself a religion. The demand that it should be is, I hold, founded upon a wrong view as to the relation between the abstract theory and the art of conduct. To convert the world you have not merely to prove your theories, but to stimulate the imagination, to discipline the passions, to provide modes of utterance for the emotions and symbols which may represent the fundamental beliefs-briefly, to do what is done by the founders of the great religions. To transmute speculation into action is a problem of tremendous difficulty, and I only glance in the briefest way at its nature. We, I take it, as members of Ethical Societies, have no claim to be, even in the humblest way, missionaries of a new religion: but are simply interested in doing what we can to discuss in a profitable way the truths which it ought to embody or reflect. But that is itself a work of no trifling importance; and we may imagine that a Bentham, refreshed by his century's slumber, and having dropped some of his little personal vanities, would on the whole be satisfied with what he saw. If Bacon could again come to life, he too would find that the methods which he contemplated and the doctrines which he preached were narrow and refutive; yet his prophecies of scientific growth have been more than realised by his successors, modifying, in some ways, rejecting his principles. And so Bentham might hold to-day that, although his sacred formula was not so exhaustive or precise as he fancied, yet the conscious and deliberate pursuit of the happiness of mankind had taken a much more important place in the aspirations of the time. He would see that the vast changes which have taken place in society, vast beyond all previous conception, were bringing up ever new problems, requiring more elaborate methods, and more systematic reasoning. He would observe that many of the abuses which he denounced have disappeared, and that though progress does not take place along the precise lines which he laid down, there is both a clearer recognition of the great ends of conduct, and a general advance in the direction which he desired. That this can be carried on by promoting a free and full discussion of first principles; that the great social evils which still exist can be diminished, and the creed of the future, however dim its outlines may be to our perception, may be purified as much as possible from ancient prejudice and superstition, is our faith; and however little we can do to help in carrying out that process, we desire to do that little.

1 Address to West London Ethical Society, 4th December, 1892.

SCIENCE AND POLITICS

2

It is with great pleasure that I address you as president of this Society. Your main purpose, as I understand, is to promote the serious study of political and social problems in a spirit purged from the prejudice and narrowness of mere party conflict. You desire, that is, to promote a scientific investigation of some of the most important topics to which the human mind can devote itself. There is no purpose of which I approve more cordially: yet the very statement suggests a doubt. To speak of science and politics together is almost to suggest irony. And if politics be taken in the ordinary sense; if we think of the discussions by which the immediate fate of measures and of ministries is decided, I should be inclined to think that they belong to a sphere of thought to which scientific thought is hardly applicable, and in which I should be personally an unwarrantable intruder. My friends have sometimes accused me, indeed, of indifference to politics. I confess that I have never been able to follow the details of party warfare with the interest which they excite in some minds: and reasons, needless to indicate, have caused me to stray further and further away from intercourse with the society in which such details excite a predominant-I do not mean to insinuate an excessive-interest. I feel that if I were to suggest any arguments bearing directly upon home rule or disestablishment, I should at once come under that damnatory epithet "academical," which so neatly cuts the ground from under the feet of the political amateur. Moreover, I recognise a good deal of justice in the implied criticism. An active politician who wishes to impress his doctrines upon his countrymen, should have a kind of knowledge to which I can make no pretension. I share the ordinary feelings of awful reverence with which the human bookworm looks up to the man of business. He has faculties which in me are rudimentary, but which I can appreciate by their contrast to my own feebleness. The "knowledge of the world" ascribed to lawyers, to politicians, financiers, and such persons, like the "knowledge of the human heart" so often ascribed to dramatists and novelists, represents, I take it, a very real kind of knowledge; but it is rather an instinct than a set of definite principles; a power of somehow estimating the tendencies and motives of their fellow-creatures in a mass by rule of thumb, rather than by any distinctly assignable logical process; only to be gained by long experience and shrewd observation of men and cities. Such a faculty, as it reaches sound results without employing explicit definitions and syllogisms and inductive processes, sometimes inclines its possessors to look down too contemptuously upon the closet student.

While, however, I frankly confess my hopeless incapacity for taking any part in the process by which party platforms are constructed, I should be ashamed to admit that I was not very keenly interested in political discussions which seem to me to touch vitally important matters. And fully recognising the vast superiority of the practical man in his own world, I also hold that he should not treat me and my like as if we, according to the famous comparison, were black beetles, and he at the opposite pole of the universe. There exists, in books at least, such a thing as political theory, apart from that claiming to underlie the immediate special applications. Your practical man is given to appealing to such theories now and then; though I confess that he too often leaves the impression of having taken them up on the spur of the moment to round a peroration and to give dignity to a popular cry; and that, in his lips, they are apt to sound so crude and artificial that one can only wonder at his condescending to notice them. He ridicules them as the poorest of platitudes whenever they are used by an antagonist, and one can only hope that his occasional homage implies that he too has a certain belief that there ought to be, and perhaps may somewhere be, a sound theory, though he has not paid it much attention. Well, we, I take it, differ from him simply in this respect, that we believe more decidedly that such theory has at least a potential existence; and that if hitherto it is a very uncertain and ambiguous guide, the mere attempt to work it out seriously may do something to strengthen and deepen our practical political convictions. A man of real ability, who is actively engaged in politics without being submerged by merely political intrigues, can hardly fail to wish at least to institute some kind of research into the principles which guide his practice. To such a desire we may attribute some very stimulating books, such, for example, as Bagehot's Physics and Politics or Mr. Bryce's philosophical study of the United States. What I propose to do is to suggest a few considerations as to the real value and proper direction of these arguments, which lie, as it were, on the borderland between the immediate "platform" and the abstract theory.

Philosophers have given us the name "Sociology"-a barbarous name, say some-for the science which deals with the subject matter of our inquiries. Is it more than a name for a science which may or may not some day come into existence? What is science? It is simply organised knowledge; that part of our knowledge which is definite, established beyond reasonable doubt, and which achieves its task by formulating what are called "scientific laws". Laws in this sense are general formulæ, which, when the necessary data are supplied, will enable us to extend our knowledge beyond the immediate facts of perception. Given a planet, moving at a given speed in a given direction, and controlled by given attractive forces, we can determine its place at a future moment. Or given a vegetable organism in a given environment, we can predict within certain limits the way in which it will grow, although the laws are too obscure and too vague to enable us to speak of it with any approach to the precision of astronomy. And we should have reached a similar stage in sociology if from a given social or political constitution adopted by a given population, we could prophesy what would be the results. I need not say that any approximation to such achievements is almost indefinitely distant. Personal claims to such powers of prediction rather tend to bring discredit upon the embryo science. Coleridge gives in the Biographia Literaria a quaint statement of his own method. On every great occurrence, he says, he tried to discover in past history the event that most nearly resembled it. He examined the original authorities. "Then fairly subtracting the points of difference from the points of likeness," as the balance favoured the former or the latter, he conjectured that the result would be the same, or different. So, for example, he was able to prophesy the end of the Spanish rising against Napoleon from the event of the war between Philip II. and the Dutch provinces. That is, he cried, "Heads!" and on this occasion the coin did not come down tails. But I need hardly point out how impossible is the process of political arithmetic. What is meant by adding or subtracting in this connection? Such a rule of three would certainly puzzle me, and, I fancy, most other observers. We may say that the insurrection of a patriotic people, when they are helped from without, and their oppressors have to operate from a distant base and to fight all Europe at the same time, will often succeed; and we may often be right; but we should not give ourselves the airs of prophets on that account. There are many superficial analogies of the same character. My predecessor, Professor Dicey, pointed out some of them, to confirm his rather depressing theory that history is nothing but an old almanac. Let me take a common one, which, I think, may illustrate our problem. There is a certain analogy between the cases of Cæsar, Cromwell, and Napoleon. In each case we have a military dictatorship as the final outcome of a civil war. Some people imagined that this analogy would apply to the United States, and that Washington or Grant would be what was called the man on horseback. The reasoning really involved was, in fact, a very simple one. The destruction of an old system of government makes some form of dictatorship the only alternative to chaos. It therefore gives a chance to the one indisputable holder of power in its most unmistakable shape, namely, to the general of a disciplined army. A soldier accordingly assumed power in each of the three first cases, although the differences between the societies ruled by the Roman, the English and the French dictators are so vast that further comparison soon becomes idle. Neither Washington nor Grant had the least chance of making themselves dictators had they wished, because the civil wars had left governments perfectly uninjured and capable of discharging all their functions, and had not produced a regular army with interests of its own. In this and other cases, I should say that such an analogy may be to some extent instructive, but I should certainly deny that there was anything like a scientific induction. We, happily, can reason to some extent upon political matters by the help of simple common sense before it has undergone that process of organisation, of reduction to precise measurable statements, which entitles it to be called a scientific procedure. The resemblance of Washington to Cromwell was of the external and superficial order. It may be compared to those analogies which exist between members of different natural orders without implying any deeper resemblance. A whale, we know, is like a fish in so far as he swims about in the sea, and he has whatever fishlike qualities are implied in the ability to swim. He will die on land, though not from the same causes. But, physiologically, he belongs to a different race, and we should make blunders if we argued from the external likeness to a closer resemblance. Or, to drop what may be too fanciful a comparison, it may be observed that all assemblies of human beings may be contrasted in respect of being numerous or select, and have certain properties in consequence. We may therefore make some true and general propositions about the contrasts between the action of small and large consultative bodies which will apply to many widely different cases. A good many, and, I think, some really valuable observations of this kind have been made, and form the substance of many generalisations laid down as to the relative advantages of democracy and aristocracy. Now I should be disposed to say that such remarks belong rather to the morphology than the physiology of the social organism. They indicate external resemblances between bodies of which the intimate constitution and the whole mode of growth and conditions of vitality, may be entirely different. Such analogies, then, though not without their value, are far from being properly scientific.

What remains? There is, shall we say, no science of sociology-merely a heap of vague, empirical observations, too flimsy to be useful in strict logical inference? I should, I confess, be apt to say so myself. Then, you may proceed, is it not idle to attempt to introduce a scientific method? And to that I should emphatically reply, No! it is of the highest importance. The question, then, will follow, how I can maintain these two positions at once. And to that I make, in the first place, this general answer: Sociology is still of necessity a very vague body of approximate truths. We have not the data necessary for obtaining anything like precise laws. A mathematician can tell you precisely what he means when he speaks of bodies moving under the influence of an attraction which varies inversely as the square of the distance. But what are the attractive forces which hold together the body politic? They are a number of human passions, which even the acutest psychologists are as yet quite unable to analyse or to classify: they act according to laws of which we have hardly the vaguest inkling; and, even if we possessed any definite laws, the facts to which they have to be applied are so amazingly complex as to defy any attempt at assigning results. There is, so far as I can see, no ground for supposing that there is or ever can be a body of precise truths at all capable of comparison with the exact sciences. But this obvious truth, though it implies very narrow limits to our hopes of scientific results, does not force us to renounce the application of scientific method. The difficulty applies in some degree even to physiology as compared with physics, as the vital phenomena are incomparably more complex than those with which we have to deal in the simpler sciences; and yet nobody doubts that a scientific physiology is a possibility, and, to some extent, a reality. Now, in sociology, however imperfect it may be, we may still apply the same methods which have been so fruitful in other departments of thought. We may undertake it in the scientific spirit which depends upon patient appeal to observation, and be guided by the constant recollection that we are dealing with an organism, the various relations of whose constituent parts are determined by certain laws to which we may, perhaps, make some approximation. We may do so, although their mutual actions and reactions are so complex and subtle that we can never hope to disentangle them with any approach to completeness. And one test of the legitimacy of our methods will be, that although we do not hope to reach any precise and definitely assignable law, we yet reach, or aim at reaching, results which, while wanting in precision, want precision alone to be capable of incorporation in an ideal science such as might actually exist for a supernatural observer of incomparably superior powers. A man who knows, though he knows nothing more, that the moon is kept in its orbit by forces similar to or identical with those which cause the fall of an apple, knows something which only requires more definite treatment to be made into a genuine theory of gravitation. If, on the contrary, he merely pays himself with words, with vague guesses about occult properties, or a supposed angel who directs the moon's course, he is still in the unscientific stage. His theory is not science still in the vague, but something which stops the way to science. Now, if we can never hope to get further than the step which in the problem of gravitation represents the first step towards science, yet that step may be a highly important one. It represents a diversion of the current of thought from such channels as end in mere shifting sands of speculation, into the channel which leads towards some definite conclusion, verifiable by experience, and leading to conclusions, not very precise, but yet often pointing to important practical results. It may, perhaps, be said that, as the change which I am supposing represents only a change of method and spirit, it can achieve no great results in actual assignable truth. Well! a change of method and spirit is, in my opinion, of considerable importance, and very vague results would still imply an improvement in the chaos of what now passes for political philosophy. I will try to indicate very briefly the kind of improvement of which we need not despair.

First of all, I conceive that, as I have indicated, a really scientific habit of thought would dispel many hopeless logomachies. When Burke, incomparably the greatest of our philosophical politicians, was arguing against the American policy of the Government, he expressed his hatred of metaphysics-the "Serbonian bog," as he called it, in which whole armies had been lost. The point at which he aimed was the fruitless discussion of abstract rights, which prevented people from applying their minds to the actual facts, and from seeing that metaphysical entities of that kind were utterly worthless when they ceased to correspond to the wants and aspirations of the peoples concerned. He could not, as he said, draw up an indictment against a nation, because he could not see how such troubles as had arisen between England and the Colonies were to be decided by technical distinctions such as passed current at nisi prius. I am afraid that the mode of reasoning condemned by Burke has not yet gone out of fashion. I do not wish to draw down upon myself the wrath of metaphysicians. I am perfectly willing that they should go on amusing themselves by attempting to deduce the first principles of morality from abstract considerations of logical affirmation and denial. But I will say this, that, in any case, and whatever the ultimate meaning of right and wrong, all political and social questions must be discussed with a continual reference to experience, to the contents as well as to the form of their metaphysical concepts. It is, to my mind, quite as idle to attempt to determine the value, say, of a political theory by reasoning independent of the character and circumstances of the nation and its constituent members, as to solve a medical question by abstract formulæ, instead of by careful, prolonged, and searching investigation into the constitution of the human body. I think that this requires to be asserted so long as popular orators continue to declaim, for example, about the "rights of man," or the doctrines of political equality. I by no means deny, or rather I should on due occasion emphatically assert, that the demands covered by such formulæ are perfectly right, and that they rest upon a base of justice. But I am forced to think that, as they are generally stated, they can lead to nothing but logomachy. When a man lays down some such sweeping principle, his real object is to save himself the trouble of thinking. So long as the first principles from which he starts are equally applicable,-and it is of the very nature of these principles that they should be equally applicable to men in all times and ages, to Englishmen and Americans, Hindoos and Chinese, Negroes and Australians,-they are worthless for any particular case, although, of course, they may be accidentally true in particular cases. In short, leaving to the metaphysicians-that is, postponing till the Greek Kalends-any decision as to the ultimate principles, I say that every political theory should be prepared to justify itself by an accurate observation of the history and all the various characteristics of the social organisation to which it is to be applied.

This points to the contrast to which I have referred: the contrast between the keen vigorous good sense upon immediate questions of the day, to which I often listen with the unfeigned admiration due to the shrewd man of business, and the paltry little outworn platitudes which he introduces when he wants to tag his arguments with sounding principles. I think, to take an example out of harm's way, that an excellent instance is found in the famous American treatise, the Federalist. It deserves all the credit it has won so long as the authors are discussing the right way to form a constitution which may satisfy the wants and appease the prejudices then actually existing. In spite of such miscalculations as beset all forecasts of the future, they show admirable good sense and clear appreciation. But when they think it necessary to appeal to Montesquieu, to tag their arguments from common sense with little ornamental formulæ learnt from philosophical writings, they show a very amiable simplicity; but they also seem to me to sink at once to the level of a clever prize essay in a university competition. The mischief may be slight when we are merely considering literary effect. But it points to a graver evil. In political discussions, the half-trained mind has strong convictions about some particular case, and then finds it easiest to justify its conviction by some sweeping general principle. It really starts, speaking in terms of logic, by assuming the truth of its minor and takes for granted that any major which will cover the minor is therefore established. Nothing saves so much trouble in thinking as the acceptance of a good sounding generality or a self-evident truth. Where your poor scientific worker plods along, testing the truth of his argument at every point, making qualifications and reservations, and admitting that every general principle may require to be modified in concrete cases, you can thus both jump to your conclusion and assume the airs of a philosopher. It is, I fancy, for this reason that people have such a tendency to lay down absolute rules about really difficult points. It is so much easier to say at once that all drinking ought to be suppressed, than to consider how, in actual circumstances, sobriety can be judiciously encouraged; and by assuming a good self-evident law and denouncing your opponents as immoral worshippers of expediency, you place yourself in an enviable position of moral dignity and inaccessibility. No argument can touch you. These abstract rules, too, have the convenience of being strangely ambiguous. I have been almost pathetically affected when I have observed how some thoroughly commonplace person plumes himself on preserving his consistency because he sticks resolutely to his party dogmas, even when their whole meaning has evaporated. Some English radicals boasted of consistency because they refused to be convinced by experience that republicans under a military dictator could become tyrannous and oppressive. At the present day, I see many worthy gentlemen, who from being thorough-going individualists, have come to swallow unconsciously the first principles of socialism without the least perception that they have changed, simply because a new meaning has been gradually insinuated into the sacred formulæ. Scientific habits of thought, I venture to suggest, would tend to free a man from the dominion of these abstract phrases, which sometimes make men push absolute dogmas to extravagant results, and sometimes blind them to the complete transformation which has taken place in their true meaning. The great test of statesmanship, it is said, is the knowledge how and when to make a compromise, and when to hold fast to a principle. The tendency of the thoughtless is to denounce all compromise as wicked, and to stick to a form of words without bothering about the real meaning. Belief in "fads"-I cannot avoid the bit of slang-and singular malleability of real convictions are sometimes generated just by want of serious thought; and, at any rate, both phenomena are very common at present.

This suggests another aspect of reasoning in a scientific spirit, namely, the importance which it attaches to a right comprehension of the practicable. The scientific view is sometimes described as fatalistic. A genuine scientific theory implies a true estimate of the great forces which mould institutions, and therefore a true apprehension of the limits within which they can be modified by any proposed change. We all remember Sydney Smith's famous illustration, in regard to the opposition to the Reform Bill, of Mrs. Partington's attempt to stop the Atlantic with her mop. Such an appeal is sometimes described as immoral. Many politicians, no doubt, find in it an excuse for immoral conduct. They assume that such and such a measure is inevitable, and therefore they think themselves justified for advocating it, even though they hold it to be wrong. Indeed, I observe that many excellent journalists are apparently unable to perceive any distinction between the assertion that a measure will be passed, and that it ought to be passed. Undoubtedly, if I think a measure unjust, I ought to say that it is unjust, even if I am sure that it will nevertheless be carried, and, in some cases, even though I may be a martyr to my opposition. If it is inevitable, it can be carried without my help, and my protest may at least sow a seed for future reaction. But this is no answer to the argument of Sydney Smith when taken in a reasonable sense. The opposition to the Reform Bill was a particular case of the opposition to the advance of democracy. The statement that democracy has advanced and will advance, is sometimes taken to be fatalistic. People who make the assertion may answer for themselves. I should answer, as I think we should all answer now, that the advance of democracy, desirable or undesirable, depended upon causes far too deep and general to be permanently affected by any Reform Bill. It was only one aspect of vast social changes which had been going on for centuries; and to propose to stop it by throwing out the Reform Bill was like proposing to stop a child's growth by forcing him to go on wearing his long clothes. Sydney Smith's answer might be immoral if it simply meant, don't fight because you will be beaten. It may often be a duty to take a beating. But it was, perhaps, rather a way of saying that if you want to stop the growth of democracy, you must begin by altering the course of the social, intellectual and moral changes which have been operating through many generations, and that unless you can do that, it is idle to oppose one particular corollary, and so to make a revolution inevitable, instead of a peaceful development. To say that any change is impossible in the absolute sense, may be fatalism; but it is simple good sense, and therefore good science, to say that to produce any change whatever you must bring to bear a force adequate to the change. When a man's leg is broken, you can't expect to heal it by a bit of sticking-plaster; a pill is not supposed, now, to be a cure for an earthquake; and to insist upon such facts is not to be fatalistic, but simply to say that a remedy must bear some proportion to an evil. It is a commonplace to observe upon the advantage which would have been gained if our grandfathers would have looked at the French Revolution scientifically. A terrible catastrophe had occurred abroad. The true moral, as we all see now, was that England should make such reforms as would obviate the danger of a similar catastrophe at home. The moral which too many people drew was too often, that all reforms should be stopped; with the result that the evils grew worse and social strata more profoundly alienated. It is a first principle of scientific reasoning, that a break-down of social order implies some antecedent defect, demanding an adequate remedy. It is a primary assumption of party argument, that the opposite party is wholly wrong, that its action is perfectly gratuitous, and either causeless or produced by the direct inspiration of the devil. The struggle, upon the scientific theory, represents two elements in an evolution which can be accomplished peacefully by such a reconstruction as will reconcile the conflicting aims and substitute harmony for discord. On the other doctrine, it is a conflict of hopelessly antagonistic principles, one of which is to be forcibly crushed.

I hope that I am not too sanguine, but I cannot help believing that in this respect we have improved, and improved by imbibing some of the scientific doctrine. I think that in recent discussions of the most important topics, however bitter and however much distorted by the old party spirit, there is yet a clearer recognition than of old, that widely-spread discontent is not a reason for arbitrary suppression, but for seeking to understand and remove its causes. We should act in the spirit of Spinoza's great saying; and it should be our aim, as it was his care, "neither to mock, to bewail, nor to denounce men's actions, but to understand them". That is equally true of men's opinions. If they are violent, passionate, subversive of all order, our duty is not bare denunciations, but a clear comprehension of the causes, not of the ostensible reasons, of their opinions, and a resolution to remove those causes. I think this view has made some way: I am sure that it will make more way if we become more scientific in spirit; and it is one of the main reasons for encouraging such a spirit. The most obvious difficulty just now is one upon which I must touch, though with some fear and trembling. A terrible weapon has lately been coming into perfection, to which its inventors have given the elegant name of a "boom". The principle is-so far as I can understand-that the right frame of mind for dealing with the gravest problems is to generate a state of violent excitement, to adopt any remedy, real or supposed, which suggests itself at the moment, and to denounce everybody who suggests difficulties as a cynic or a cold-blooded egoist; and therefore to treat grave chronic and organic diseases of society by spasmodic impulses, to make stringent laws without condescending to ask whether they will work, and try the boldest experiments without considering whether they are likely to increase or diminish the evil. This, as some people think, is one of the inevitable consequences of democracy. I hope that it is not; but if it is, it is one of the inevitable consequences against which we, as cultivators of science, should most seriously protest, in the hope that we may some day find Philip sober enough to consider the consequences of his actions under the influence of spiritual intoxication. Professor Huxley, in one of those smart passages of arms which so forcibly illustrated his intellectual vigour, gave an apologue, which I wish that I could steal without acknowledgment. He spoke of an Irish carman who, on being told that he was not going in the right direction, replied that he was at any rate going at a great pace. The scientific doctrine is simply that we should look at the map before we set out for Utopia; and I think that a doctrine which requires to be enforced by every means in our power.

This tendency, of course, comes out prominently in the important discussions of social and economic problems. That is a matter upon which I cannot now dwell, and which has been sufficiently emphasised by many eminent writers. If modern orators confined themselves to urging that the old economists exaggerated their claims to scientific accuracy, and were, in point of fact, guilty of many logical errors and hasty generalisations, I, at least, could fully agree with them. But the general impression seems to be, that because the old arguments were faulty, all argument is irrelevant: that because the alleged laws of nature were wrongly stated, there are no laws of nature at all; and that we may proceed to rearrange society, to fix the rate of wages or the rent of land or the incomes of capitalists without any reference at all to the conditions under which social arrangements have been worked out and actually carried on. This is, in short, to sanction the most obvious weakness of popular movements, and to assure the ignorant and thoughtless that they are above reason, and their crude guesses infallible guides to truth.

One view which tries to give some plausibility to these assumptions is summed up in the now current phrase about the "masses" and the "classes". We all know the regular process of logical fence of the journalist, i.e., thrust and parry, which is repeated whenever such questions turn up. The Radical calls his opponent Tory and reactionary. The wicked Tory, it is said, thinks only of the class interest; believes that the nation exists for the sake of the House of Lords; lives in a little citadel provided with all the good things, which he is ready to defend against every attempt at a juster distribution; selfishness is his one motive; repression by brute force his only theory of government; and his views of life in general are those of the wicked cynics who gaze from their windows in Pall Mall. Then we have the roll of all the abuses which have been defended by this miscreant and his like since the days of George III.-slavery and capital punishment, and pensions and sinecures, and protection and the church establishment. The popular instinct, it is urged, has been in the right in so many cases that there is an enormous presumption in favour of the infallibility of all its instincts. The reply, of course, is equally obvious. Your boast, says the Conservative, that you please the masses, is in effect a confession that you truckle to the mob. You mean that your doctrines spread in proportion to the ignorance of your constituents. You prove the merits of your theories by showing that they disgust people the more they think. The Liberalism of a district, it has been argued, varies with the number of convictions for drunkenness. If it be easy to denounce our ancestors, it is also easy to show how they built up the great empire which now shelters us; and how, if they had truckled, as you would have us truckle, to popular whims, we should have been deprived of our commerce, our manufactures, and our position in the civilised world. And then it is easy to produce a list of all the base demagogues who have misled popular impatience and ignorance from the days of Cleon to those of the French Convention, or of the last disreputable "boss" bloated with corruption and the plunder of some great American city. This is the result, it is suggested, of pandering to the mob, and generally ostracising the intelligent citizen.

I merely sketch the familiar arguments which any journalist has ready at hand, and, by a sufficient spice of references to actual affairs, can work up into any number of pointed leading articles. I will only observe that such arguments seem to me to illustrate that curious unreality of political theories of which I have spoken. It seems to be tacitly assumed on both sides, that votes are determined by a process of genuine reasoning. One side may be ignorant and the other prejudiced; but the arguments I have recapitulated seem to imply the assumption that the constituents really reflect upon the reasons for and against the measures proposed, and make up their minds accordingly. They are spoken of as though they were a body of experts, investigating a scientific doctrine, or at least a jury guided by the evidence laid before them. Upon that assumption, as it seems to me, the moral would be that the whole system is a palpable absurdity. The vast majority of voters scarcely think at all, and would be incapable of judging if they did. Hundreds of thousands care more for Dr. Grace's last score or the winner of the Derby than for any political question whatever. If they have opinions, they have neither the training nor the knowledge necessary to form any conclusion whatever. Consider the state of mind of the average voter-of nine men out of ten, say, whom you meet in the Strand. Ask yourselves honestly what value you would attach to his opinion upon any great question-say, of foreign politics or political economy. Has he ever really thought about them? Is he superficially acquainted with any of the relevant facts? Is he even capable of the imaginative effort necessary to set before him the vast interests often affected? And would the simple fact that he said "Yes" to a given question establish in your mind the smallest presumption against the probability that the right answer would be "No"? What are the chances that a majority of people, of whom not one in a hundred has any qualifications for judging, will give a right judgment? Yet that is the test suggested by most of the conventional arguments on both sides; for I do not say this as intending to accept the anti-democratic application. It is just as applicable, I believe, to the educated and the well-off. I need not labour the point, which is sufficiently obvious. I am quite convinced that, for example, the voters for a university will be guided by unreasonable prejudices as the voters for a metropolitan constituency. In some ways they will be worse. To find people who believe honestly in antiquated prejudices, you must go to the people who have been trained to believe them. An ecclesiastical seminary can manage to drill the pupils into professing absurdities from which average common sense would shrink, and only supply logical machinery for warring against reason. The reference to enlightened aristocracies is common enough; but I cannot discover that, "taken in a lump," any particular aristocracy cannot be as narrow-minded, short-sighted, and selfish, as the most rampant democracy. In point of fact, we all know that political action is determined by instinct rather than by reason. I do not mean that instinct is opposed to reason: it is simply a crude, undeveloped, inarticulate form of reason; it is blended with prejudices for which no reason is assigned, or even regarded as requisite. Such blind instincts, implying at most a kind of groping after error, necessarily govern the majority of men of all classes, in political as in other movements. The old apologists used to argue on the hypothesis that men must have accepted Christianity on the strength of a serious inquiry into the evidences. The fallacy of the doctrine is sufficiently plain: they accepted it because it suited them on the whole, and was fitted, no doubt, to their intellectual needs, but was also fitted to their emotional and moral needs as developed under certain social conditions. The inference from the general acceptance of any theory is not that it is true, but that it is true enough to satisfy the very feeble demand for logic-that it is not palpably absurd or self-contradictory; and that, for some reason or other, it satisfies also the imagination, the affections, and the aspirations of the believers. Not to go into other questions, this single remark indicates, I think, the attitude which the scientific observer would adopt in regard to this ancient controversy. He would study the causes as well as the alleged reasons assignable for any general instinct, and admit that its existence is one of the primary data which have to be taken into account. To denounce democracy or aristocracy is easy enough; and it saves trouble to assume that God is on one side and the devil on the other. The true method, I take it, is that which was indicated by Tocqueville's great book upon democracy in America; a book which, if I may trust my own impressions, though necessarily imperfect as regards America, is a perfectly admirable example of the fruitful method of studying such problems. Though an aristocrat by birth and breeding, Tocqueville had the wisdom to examine democratic beliefs and institutions in a thoroughly impartial spirit; and, instead of simply denouncing or admiring, to trace the genesis of the prevalent ideas and their close connection with the general state of social development. An inquiry conducted in that spirit would not lead to the absolute dogmatic conclusions in which the superficial controversialist delights. It would show, perhaps, that there was at least this much truth in the democratic contention, that the masses are, by their position, exempt from some of the prejudices which are ingrained in the members of a smaller caste; that they are therefore more accessible to certain moral considerations, and more anxious to promote the greatest happiness of the greater number. But it might also show how the weakness of the ignorant and untrained mind produces the characteristic evils of sentimentalism and impatience, of a belief in the omnipotence of legislation, and an excessive jealousy of all superiorities; and might possibly, too, exhibit certain merits which are impressed upon the aristocrat by his sense of the obligations of nobility. I do not in the least mean to express any opinion about such questions; I desire only to indicate the temper in which I conceive that they should be approached.

I have lived long enough to be utterly unable to believe-though some older politicians than I seem still to believe, especially on the eve of a dissolution-that any of our party lines coincide with the lines between good and bad, wise and foolish. Every one, of course, will repudiate the abstract theory. Yet we may notice how constantly it is assumed; and can see to what fallacies it leads when we look for a moment at the historical questions which no longer unite party feeling. Few, indeed, even of our historians, can write without taking party views of such questions. Even the candid and impartial seem to deserve these epithets chiefly because they want imagination, and can cast blame or applaud alternately, because they do not enter into the real spirit of either party. Their views are sometimes a medley of inconsistent theories, rather than a deeper view which might reconcile apparent inconsistencies. I will only mention one point which often strikes me, and may lead to a relevant remark. Every royalist historian, we all know, labours to prove that Charles I. was a saint, and Cromwell a hypocrite. The view was natural at the time of the civil wars; but it now should suggest an obvious logical dilemma. If the monarchical theory which Charles represented was sound, and Charles was also a wise and good man, what caused the rebellion? A perfect man driving a perfect engine should surely not have run it off the rails. The royalist ought to seek to prove that Charles was a fool and a knave, to account for the collapse of royalty; and the case against royalty is all the stronger, if you could show that Charles, in spite of impeccable virtue, was forced by his position to end on the scaffold. Choose between him and the system which he applied. So Catholics and conservatives are never tired of denouncing Henry VIII. and the French revolutionists. So far as I can guess (I know very little about it), their case is a very strong one. I somehow believe, in spite of Froude, that Henry VIII. was a tyrant; and eulogies upon the reign of terror generally convince me that a greater set of scoundrels seldom came to the surface, than the perpetrators of those enormities. But then the real inference is, to my mind, very different. Henry VIII. was the product of the previous time; the ultimate outcome of that ideal state of things in which the church had its own way during the ages of truth. Must not the system have been wrong, when it had so lost all moral weight as to be at the mercy of a ruffianly plunderer? And so, as we all admit now, the strongest condemnation of the old French régime is the fact that it had not only produced such a set of miscreants as those who have cast permanent odium even upon sound principles; but that its king and rulers went down before them without even an attempt at manly resistance. A revolution does not, perhaps, justify itself; it does not prove that its leaders judged rightly and acted virtuously: but, beyond a doubt, it condemns the previous order which brought it about. What a horrid thing is the explosion! Why, is the obvious answer, did you allow the explosive materials to accumulate, till the first match must fire the train? The greatest blot upon Burke, I need hardly say, is that his passions blinded him in his age, to this, as we now see, inevitable conclusion.

The old-fashioned view, I fancy, is a relic of that view of history in which all the great events and changes were personified in some individual hero. The old "legislators," Lycurgus and Solon and the like, were supposed to have created the institutions which were really the products of a slow growth. When a favourable change due to economical causes took place in the position of the French peasantry, the peasants, says Michelet somewhere, called it "good king Henry". Carlyle's theory of hero worship is partly an application of the same mode of thought. You embody your principle in some concrete person; canonise him or damn him, as he represents truth or error; and take credit to yourself for insight and for a lofty morality. It becomes a kind of blasphemy to suggest that your great man, who thus stands for an inspired leader dropped straight out of heaven, was probably at best very imperfect, one-sided, and at least as much of a product as a producer. The crudity of the method is even regarded as a proof of its morality. Your common-place moralist likes to call everything black or white; he despises all qualifications as casuistical refinements, and plumes himself on the decisive verdict, saint or sinner, with which he labels the adherents and opponents of his party. And yet we know as a fact, how absurd are such judgments. We know how men are betrayed into bad causes from good motives, or put on the right side because it happens to harmonise with their lower interests. Saints-so we are told-have been the cruellest persecutors; and kings, acting from purely selfish ambition, have consolidated nations or crushed effete and mischievous institutions. If we can make up our minds as to which was, on the whole, the best cause,-and, generally speaking, both sides represented some sound principle,-it does not follow that it was also the cause of all the best men. Before we can judge of the individual, we must answer a hundred difficult questions: If he took the right side, did he take it from the right motives? Was it from personal ambition or pure patriotism? Did he see what was the real question at issue? Did he foresee the inevitable effect of the measures which he advocated? If he did not see, was it because he was human, and therefore short-sighted; or because he was brutal, and therefore wanting in sympathy; or because he had intellectual defects, which made it impossible for him to escape from the common illusions of the time? These, and any number of similar difficulties, arise when we try to judge of the great men who form landmarks in our history, from the time of Boadicea to that of Queen Victoria. They are always amusing, and sometimes important; but there is always a danger that they may warp our views of the vital facts. The beauty of Mary Queen of Scots still disqualifies many people from judging calmly the great issues of a most important historical epoch. I will leave it to you to apply this to our views of modern politics, and judge the value of the ordinary assumption which assumes that all good men must be on one side. Now we may say that the remedy for such illusions points to the importance of a doctrine which is by no means new, but which has, I think, bearings not always recognised. We have been told, again and again, since Plato wrote his Republic, that society is an organism. It is replied that this is at best an analogy upon which too great stress must not be laid; and we are warned against the fanciful comparisons which some writers have drawn between the body corporate and the actual physical body, with its cells, tissues, nervous system, and so forth. Now, whatever may be the danger of that mode of reasoning, I think that the statement, properly understood, corresponds to a simple logical canon too often neglected in historical and political reasonings. It means, I take it, in the first place, that every man is a product as well as a producer; that there is no such thing as the imaginary individual with fixed properties, whom theorists are apt to take for granted as the base of their reasoning; that no man or group of men is intelligible without taking into account the mass of instincts transmitted through their predecessors, and therefore without referring to their position in the general history of human development. And, secondly, it is essential to remember in speaking of any great man, or of any institution, their position as parts of a complicated system of actions and emotions. The word "if," I may say, changes its meaning. "If" Harold had won the battle of Hastings, what would have been the result? The answer would be comparatively simple, if we could, in the old fashion, attribute to William the Conqueror all the results in which he played a conspicuous part: if, therefore, we could make out a definite list of effects of which he was the cause, and, by simply "deducting" them, after Coleridge's fashion, from the effects which actually followed, determine what was the precise balance. But when we consider how many causes were actually in operation, how impossible it is to disentangle and separate them, and say this followed from that, and that other from something else, we have to admit that the might have been is simply indiscoverable. The great man may have hastened what was otherwise inevitable; he may simply have supplied the particular point, round which a crystallisation took place of forces which would have otherwise discovered some other centre; and the fact that he succeeded in establishing certain institutions or laws may be simply a proof that he saw a little more clearly than others the direction towards which more general causes were inevitably propelling the nation. Briefly, we cannot isolate the particular "cause" in this case, and have to remember at every moment that it was only one factor in a vast and complex series of changes, which would no doubt have taken a different turn without it, but of which it may be indefinitely difficult to say what was the precise deflection due to its action. In trying to indicate the importance, I have had to dwell upon the difficulty, of applying anything like scientific methods to political problems. I shall conclude by trying once more to indicate why, in spite of this, I hold that the attempt is desirable, and may be fruitful.

People sometimes say that scientific methods are inapplicable because we cannot try experiments in social matters. I remember being long ago struck by a remark of Dr. Arnold, which has some bearing upon this assertion. He observed upon the great advantage possessed by Aristotle in the vast number of little republics in his time, each of which was virtually an experiment in politics. I always thought that this was fallacious somehow, and I fancy that it is not hard to indicate the general nature of the fallacy. Freeman, upon whose services to thorough and accurate study of history I am unworthy to pronounce an eulogy, fell into the same fallacy, I fancy, when he undertook to write a history of Federal Governments. He fancied that because the Achæan League and the Swiss Cantons and the United States of America all had this point in common, and that they represented the combinations of partially independent States, their history would be in a sense continuous. The obvious consideration that the federations differed in every possible way, in their religions and state of civilisation and whole social structure, might be neglected. Freeman's tendency to be indifferent to everything which was not in the narrowest sense political led him to this-as it seems to me-pedantic conception. If the prosperity of a nation depended exclusively upon the form of its government, Aristotle, as Arnold remarks, would have had before him a greater number of experiments than the modern observer. But the assumption is obviously wrong. Every one of these ancient States depended for its prosperity upon a vast number of conditions-its race, its geographical position, its stage of development, and so forth, quite impossible to tabulate or analyse; and the form of government which suited one would be entirely inapplicable to another. To extricate from all these conflicting elements the precise influence due to any institutions would be a task beyond the powers of any number of philosophers; and indeed the perplexity would probably be increased by the very number of experiments. To make an experiment fruitful, it is necessary to eliminate all the irrelevant elements which intrude into the concrete cases spontaneously offered by nature, and, for example, to obtain two cases differing only in one element, to which we may therefore plausibly attribute other contrasts. Now, the history of a hundred or a thousand small States would probably only present the introduction of new and perplexing elements for every new case. The influence, again, of individuals, or accident of war, or natural catastrophes, is greater in proportion as the State is smaller, and therefore makes it more difficult to observe the permanent and underlying influences. It seems to me, therefore, that the study, say of

English history, where we have a continuous growth over many centuries, where the disturbing influences of individuals or chance are in a greater degree cancelled by the general tendencies working beneath them, we have really a far more instructive field for political observation. This may help us to see what are the kinds of results which may be anticipated from sociological study undertaken in a serious spirit. The growth, for example, of the industrial system of England is a profoundly interesting subject of inquiry, to which we are even now only beginning to do justice. Historians have admitted, even from the time of Hume, that the ideal history should give less of mere battles and intrigues, and more account of those deeper and more continuous processes which lie, so to speak, beneath the surface. They have hardly, I think, even yet realised the full bearing and importance of this observation. Yet, of late, much has been done, though much still remains to do, in the way of a truly scientific study of the development of institutions, political, ecclesiastical, industrial, and so forth, of this and other countries. As this tendency grows, we may hope gradually to have a genuine history of the English people; an account-not of the virtues and vices of Mary Queen of Scots, or arguments as to the propriety of cutting off Charles I.'s head-but a trustworthy account of the way in which the actual structure of modern society has been developed out of its simpler germs. The biographies of great kings and generals, and so forth, will always be interesting; but to the genuine historian of the future they will be interesting not so much as giving room for psychological analyses or for dramatic portraits, but as indications of the great social forces which produced them, and the direction of which at the moment may be illustrated by their cases. I have spoken of the history of our industrial system. To know what was the position of the English labourer at various times, how it was affected by the political changes or by the great mechanical discoveries, to observe what grievances arose, what remedies were applied or sought to be applied, and with what result,-to treat all this with due reference to the whole social and intellectual evolution of which it formed a part, may well call forth the powers of our acutest and most thoroughgoing inquirers, and will, when it is done, give essential data for some of the most vitally important problems of the day. This is what I understand by an application of the scientific spirit to social and political problems. We cannot try experiments, it is said, in historical questions. We cannot help always trying experiments, and experiments of vast importance. Every man has to try an experiment upon himself when he chooses his career; and the results are frequently very unpleasant, though very instructive. We have to be our own experiments. Every man who sets up in business tries an experiment, ending in fortune or in bankruptcy. Every strike is an experiment, and generally a costly one. Every attempt at starting a new charitable organisation, or a new system of socialism or co-operation, is an experiment. Every new law is an experiment, rash or otherwise. And from all these experiments we do at least collect a certain number of general observations, which, though generally consigned to copybooks, are not without value. What is true, however, is that we cannot try such experiments as a man of science can sometimes try in his laboratory, where he can select and isolate the necessary elements in any given process, and decide, by subjecting them to proper conditions, how a definite question is to be answered. Our first experiments are all in the rough, so to speak, tried at haphazard, and each involving an indefinite number of irrelevant conditions. But there is a partial compensation. We cannot tabulate the countless experiments which have been tried with all their distracting varieties. Yet in a certain sense the answer is given for us. For the social structure at any period is in fact the net product of all the experiments that have been made by the individuals of which it is and has been composed. Therefore, so far as we can obtain some general views of the successive changes in social order which have been gradually and steadily developing themselves throughout the more noisy and conspicuous but comparatively superficial political disturbances, we can detect the true meaning of some general phenomena in which the actors themselves were unconscious of the determining causes. We can see more or less what were the general causes which have led to various forms of associations, to the old guilds, or the modern factory system, to the trades unions or the co-operative societies; and correcting and verifying our general results by a careful examination of the particular instances, approximate, vaguely it may be and distantly, to some such conception of the laws of development of different social tissues as, if not properly scientific, may yet belong to the scientific order of thought. Thus, when distracted by this or that particular demand, by promises of the millennium to be inaugurated to-morrow by an Act of Parliament, or threats of some social cataclysm to overwhelm us if we concede an inch to wicked agitators, we may succeed in placing ourselves at a higher point of view, from which it is possible to look over wider horizons, to regard what is happening to-day in its relations to slow processes of elaboration, and to form judgments based upon wide and systematic inquiry, which, if they do not entitle us to predict particular events, as an astronomer predicts an eclipse, will at least be a guide to sane and sober minds, and suggest at once a humbler appreciation of what is within our power, and-I think also-a more really hopeful anticipation of genuine progress in the future.

All scientific inquiry is an interrogation of nature. We have, in Bacon's grand sententious phrase, to command nature by obeying. We learn what are the laws of social growth by living them. The great difficulty of the interrogation is to know what questions we are to put. Under the guidance of metaphysicians, we have too often asked questions to which no answer is conceivable, like children, who in first trying to think, ask, why are we living in the nineteenth century, why is England an island, or why does pain hurt, or why do two and two make four? The only answer is by giving the same facts in a different set of words, and that is a kind of answer to which metaphysical dexterity sometimes gives an air of plausibility. More frequently our ingenuity takes the form of sanctioning preconceived prejudices, by wrapping up our conclusion in our premisses, and then bringing it out triumphantly with the air of a rigorous deduction. The progress of social science implies, in the first place, the abandonment of the weary system of hunting for fruitful truths in the region of chimeras, and trying to make empty logical concepts do the work of observation of facts. It involves, again, a clear perception of the kind of questions which can be profitably asked, and the limits within which an answer, not of the illusory kind, can really be expected. And then we may come to see that, without knowing it, we have really been trying a vast and continuous experiment, since the race first began to be human. We have, blindly and unconsciously, constructed a huge organism which does, somehow or other, provide a great many millions of people with a tolerable amount of food and comfort. We have accomplished this, I say, unconsciously; for each man, limited to his own little sphere, and limited to his own interests, and guided by his own prejudices and passions, has been as ignorant of more general tendencies as the coral insect of the reef which it has helped to build. To become distinctly conscious of what it is that we have all been doing all this time, is one step in advance. We have obeyed in ignorance; and as obedience becomes conscious, we may hope, within certain narrow limits, to command, or, at least, to direct. An enlarged perception of what have been the previous results may enable us to see what results are possible, and among them to select what may be worthy ends. It is not to be supposed that we shall ever get beyond the need of constant and careful experiment. But, in proportion as we can cultivate the right frame of mind, as each member of society requires wider sympathies and a larger horizon, it is permissible to hope that the experiments may become more intelligent; that we shall not, as has so often been done, increase poverty by the very remedies which are intended to remove it, or diverge from the path of steady progressive development, into the chase of some wild chimera, which requires for its achievement only the radical alteration of all the data of experience. "Annihilate space and time, and make two lovers happy," was the modest petition of an enthusiast; and he would probably have been ready to join in the prayer, "make all men angels, and then we shall have a model society". Although in saying this my immediate moral is to preach sobriety, I do not intend to denounce enthusiasm, but to urge a necessity of organising enthusiasm. I only recommend people not to venture upon flying machines before they have studied the laws of mechanics; but I earnestly hope that some day we may be able to call a balloon as we now call a cab. To point out the method, and to admit that it is not laborious, is not to discourage aspiration, but to look facts in the face: not to preach abandonment of enthusiasm, but to urge that enthusiasm should be systematic, should lead men to study the conditions of success, and to make a bridge before they leap the gulf.

2 Address to the Social and Political Education League, 29th March, 1892.

THE SPHERE OF POLITICAL ECONOMY

There seem to be at present many conflicting views as to the nature of Political Economy. There is a popular impression that Political Economy, or, at any rate, the so-called "classical" doctrine, the doctrine which was made most definite by Ricardo, and accepted with modifications by J. S. Mill, is altogether exploded. Their main doctrines, it is suggested, were little better than mares' nests, and we may set aside their pretensions to have founded an exact science. What, then, is to come in its place? Are we simply to admit that there is no certainty about economical problems, and to fall back upon mere empiricism? Everything,-shall we say?-is to be regarded as an open question. That is, perhaps, a common impression in the popular mind. Yet, on the other hand, we may find some very able thinkers applying mathematical formulæ to economics; and that seems to suppose, that within a certain region they obtain results comparable in precision and accuracy to those of the great physical sciences. The topic is a very wide one; and it would be presumptuous in me to speak dogmatically. I wish, however, to suggest certain considerations which may, perhaps, be worth taking into account; and, as I must speak briefly, I must not attempt to supply all the necessary qualifications. I can only attempt to indicate what seems to me to be the correct point of view, and apologise if I appear to speak too dogmatically, simply because I cannot waste time by expressions of diffidence, by reference to probable criticisms, or even by a full statement of my own reasons.

A full exposition would have to define the sphere of Political Economy by describing its data and its methods. What do we assume, and how do we reason? A complete answer to these questions would indicate the limits within which we can hope for valid conclusions. I will first refer, briefly, to a common statement of one theory advocated by the old-fashioned or classical school. Economic doctrine, they have said, supposes a certain process of abstraction. We have to do with what has been called the "economic man". He is not, happily, the real man. He is an imaginary being, whose sole principle of action is to buy in the cheapest and sell in the dearest market: a man, more briefly, who always prefers a guinea-even a dirty guinea-to a pound of the cleanest. Economists reply to the remonstrances of those who deny the existence of such a monster, by adding that they do not for a moment suppose that men in general, or even tradesmen or stockbrokers, are in reality such beings,-mere money-making machines, stripped bare of all generous or altruistic sentiment-but simply that, as a matter of fact, most people do, ceteris paribus, prefer a guinea to a pound; and that so large a part of our industrial activity is carried on from motives of this kind, that we may obtain a fair approximation to the actual course of affairs by considering them as the sole motives. We shall not go wrong, for example, in financial questions, by assuming that the sole motive of speculators in the Stock Exchange is the desire to make money. Now, it is possible, perhaps, to justify this way of putting the case, by certain qualifications. I think, however, that, if strictly interpreted, it is apt to cover a serious fallacy. The "economic man" theory, we may say, assumes too much in one direction, and too little in another. It assumes too much if it is understood as implying that the desire for wealth is a purely selfish desire. A man may desire to make money in order simply to gratify his own sensual appetites. But he may also desire to be independent; and that may include a desire to do his part in the work of society, and probably does include some desire to relieve others of a burden. The wish to be self-supporting is not necessarily or purely "selfish". And obviously, too, one great motive in all such occupations is the desire to support a family, and one main inducement to saving is the desire to support it after your own death. Remove such motives, and half the impulses to regular industrial energy of all kinds would be destroyed. We must, therefore, give our "economic man" credit for motives referring to many interests besides those which he buttons into his own waistcoat. And therefore, too, as I have said, the assumption is insufficient. The very conception of economic science supposes all that is supposed, in the growth of a settled order of society. The purest type of the "economic man," as he is sometimes described, would be realised in the lowest savage, as sometimes described, who is absolutely selfish, who knocks his child on the head because it cries, and eats his aged parent if he cannot find a supply of roots. But such a being could only form herds, not societies. Political Economy only becomes conceivable when we suppose certain institutions to have been developed. It assumes, obviously, and in the first place, the institution of property; it becomes applicable, with less qualification, in proportion to the growth of the corresponding sentiments; it takes for granted all that highly elaborate set of instincts which induce me, when I want something, to produce an equivalent in exchange for it, instead of going out to take it by force. The more thorough the respect for property, the more applicable are rules of economics; and that respect implies a long training in that sense of other people's rights, which, unfortunately, is by no means so perfect as might be desired.

It follows, then, that the economist really assumes more-and rightly assumes more-than he sometimes claims. He assumes what Adam Smith assumed at the opening of his great treatise: that is, the division of labour. But the division of labour implies the organisation of society. It implies that one man is growing corn while another is digging gold, because each is confident that he will be able to exchange the products of his own labour for the products of the other man's labour. This, of course, implies settled order, respect for contracts, the preservation of peace, and the abolition of force throughout the area occupied by the society. And this, again, is only possible in so far as certain political and ecclesiastical and military institutions have been definitely constructed. The economic assumption is really an assumption-not of a certain psychological condition of the average man, but-of the existence of a certain social mechanism. A complete science would clear up fully a problem which must occur often to all of us: How do you account for London? How is it that four or five millions of people manage to subsist on an area of a few square miles, which itself produces nothing? that other millions all over the world are engaged in providing for their wants? that food and clothes and fuel, in sufficient quantities to preserve life, are being distributed with tolerable regularity to each unit in this vast and apparently chaotic crowd? and that, somehow or other, we struggle on, well or ill, by the help of a gigantic commissariat, performing functions incomparably more complex than were ever needed for military purposes? The answer supposes that there is, as a matter of fact, a great industrial organisation which discharges the various functions of producing, exchanging, distributing, and so forth; and that its mutual relations are just as capable of being investigated and stated as the relations between different parts of an army. The men and officers do not wear uniforms; they are not explicitly drilled or subject to a definite code of discipline; and their rates of pay are not settled by any central authority. But there are capitalists, "undertakers" and labourers, merchants and retail dealers and contractors, and so forth, just as certainly as there are generals and privates, horse, foot, and artillery; and their mutual relations are equally definable. The economist has to explain the working of this industrial mechanism; and the thought may sometimes occur to us, that it is strange that he should find the task so difficult. Since we ourselves have made, or at any rate constitute, the mechanism, why should it be so puzzling to find out what it is? We are cooperating in a systematic production and distribution of wealth, and we surely ought not to find any impenetrable mystery in discovering what it is that we are doing every day of our lives. Certain economists writing within this century have often been credited with the discovery of the true theory of rent, or, which is equally good for my purpose, of starting a false theory. Yet landowners and agents had been letting farms and houses for generations; and surely they ought to have known what it was that they were themselves doing. One explanation of the difficulty is, that whereas an army is constituted by certain regulations of a central authority, the industrial army has grown up unconsciously and spontaneously. Its multitudinous members have only looked each at his own little circle; the labourer only thinks of his wages, and the capitalist of his profits, without considering his relations to the whole system of which he forms a part. The peasant drives his plough for wages, and buys his tea as if the tea fell like manna from the skies, without thinking of the curious relation into which he is thus brought with the natives of another hemisphere. The order which results from all these independent activities appeared to the older economists as an illustration of the doctrine of Final Causes. Providence had so ordered things that each man, by pursuing his own interests, pursued the interests of all. To a later school it appears rather as an illustration of the doctrine by which organisms are constructed through the struggle for existence and the survival of the fittest. In either case, it seems as though the mechanism were made rather for us than by us; that it is the product of conditions which we cannot control, instead of being an arrangement put together by conscious volitions. And, therefore, when the economist shows us what in fact are the existing arrangements and their mutual relations, he appears to be making a discovery of a scientific fact as much as if he were describing the anatomy of some newly-discovered animal or plant.

The real assumption of the economist therefore is, as I think, simply the existence of a certain industrial organisation, which has a real existence as much as an army or a church; and there is no reason why his description should not be as accurate as the complexity of the facts allows. He is giving us the anatomy of society considered as a huge mechanism for producing and distributing wealth, and he makes an abstraction only in the sense that he is considering one set of facts at a time. The military writer would describe the constitution of an army without going into the psychological or political conditions which are of course implied, and without considering the soldiers in any other relations than those implied in their military services. In the same way, the economist describes the army of industry, and classifies its constituent parts. In order to explain their mutual relations, he has to make certain further assumptions, of which it would be rash to attempt a precise summary. He assumes as a fact, what has of course always been known, that scarcity implies dearness and plenty cheapness; that commodities flow to the markets where they will fetch the highest prices; that there is a certain gravitation towards equalisation of profits among capitalists, and of wages among labourers; so that capital or labour will flow towards the employments in which they will secure the highest reward. He endeavours to give the greatest accuracy to such formulæ, of which nobody, so far as I know, denies a certain approximate truth. So long as they hold good, his inferences, if logically drawn, will also hold good. They take for granted certain psychological facts, such as are implied in all statements about human nature. But the economist, as an economist, is content to take them for granted without investigating the ultimate psychological laws upon which they depend. Those laws, or rather their results, are a part of his primary data, although he may go so far into psychological problems as to try to state them more accurately. The selfishness or unselfishness of the economic man has to be considered by the psychologist or by the moralist; but the economist has only to consider their conclusions so far as they affect the facts. So long as it is true, for example, that scarcity causes dearness, that profits attract capital, that demand and supply tend to equalise each other, and so forth, his reasonings are justified; and the further questions of the ethical and psychological implications of these facts must be treated by a different science. The question of the play of economic forces thus generally reduces itself to a problem which may be thus stated: What are the conditions of industrial equilibrium? How must prices, rates of wages, and profit be related in order that the various classes concerned may receive such proportions of produce as are compatible with the maintenance of the existing system of organisation? If any specified change occurs, if production becomes easier or more difficult, if a tax be imposed, or a regulation of any kind affects previous conditions, what changes will be necessary to restore the equilibrium? These are the main problems of Political Economy. To solve, or attempt to solve them, we have to describe accurately the existing mechanism, and to suppose that it will regulate itself on the assumption which I have indicated as to demand and supply, the flow of capital and labour, and so forth. To go beyond these assumptions, and to justify them by psychological and other considerations, may be and is a most interesting task, but it takes us beyond the sphere of Economics proper.

I must here diverge for a little, to notice the view of the school of economists which seems to regard scientific accuracy as attainable by a different path. Jevons, its most distinguished leader in England, says roundly, that political science must be a "mathematical science," because "it deals throughout with quantities"; and we have been since provided with a number of formulæ, corresponding to this doctrine. The obvious general reply would be, that Political Economy cannot be an exact science because it also deals throughout with human desires. The objection is not simply that our data are too vague. That objection, as Jevons says, would, perhaps, apply to meteorology, of which nobody doubts that it is capable of being made an exact science. But why does nobody doubt that meteorology might become an exact science? Because we are convinced that all the data which would be needed are expressible in precise terms of time and space; we have to do with volumes, and masses, and weights, and forces which can be exactly measured by lines; and, in short, with things which could be exactly measured and counted. The data are, at present, insufficiently known, and possibly the problems which would result might be too complex for our powers of calculation. Still, if we could once get the data, we could express all relevant considerations by precise figures and numbers.

Now, is this true of economic science? Within certain limits, it is apparently true: Ricardo used mathematical formulæ, though he kept to arithmetic, instead of algebra. When Malthus spoke of arithmetical and geometrical ratios, the statement, true or false, was, of course, capable of precise numerical expression, so soon as the ratios were assigned. So there was the famous formula proving a relation between the number of quarters of corn produced by a given harvest, and the number of shillings that would be given for a quarter of corn. If, again, we took the number of marriages corresponding to a given price of corn, we should obtain a formula connecting the number of marriages with the number of quarters of corn produced. The utility of statistics, of course, depends upon the fact that we do empirically discover some tolerably constant and simple numerical formulæ. Such statistical statements are useful, indeed, not only in economical, but in other inquiries, which are clearly beyond the reach of mathematics. The proportion of criminals in a given population, the number of suicides, or of illegitimate births, may throw some light upon judicial and political, and even religious or ethical problems. Nor are such formulæ useless simply because empirical. The law of gravitation, for example, is empirical. Nobody knows the cause of the observed tendency of bodies to gravitate to each other, and therefore no one can say how far the law which represents the tendency must be universal. Still, the fact that, so far as we have observed, it is invariably verified, and that calculations founded upon it enable us to bring a vast variety of phenomena under a single rule, is quite enough to justify astronomical calculation.

If, therefore, we could find a mathematical formula which was, as a matter of fact, verifiable in economical problems about prices, and so forth, we should rightly apply to mathematicians to help us with their methods. But, not only do we not find any such simple relations, but we can see conclusive reasons for being sure that we can never find them. Take, for example, the case of the number of marriages under given conditions. I need hardly say that it is impossible for the ablest mathematician to calculate whether the individual A will marry the individual B. But, by taking averages, and so eliminating individual eccentricities, he might discover that, in a given country and at a given time, a rise of prices will diminish marriages in certain proportion. Our knowledge of human nature is sufficient to make that highly probable. But our knowledge also shows that such a change will act differently in different cases: there will be one formula for France, and another for England; one for Lancashire, and another for Cornwall; one for the rich, and another for the poor; and both the total wealth of a country and its distribution will affect the rule. Differences of national temperament, of political and social constitution, of religion and ecclesiastical organisation, will all have an effect; and, therefore, a formula true here and now must, in all probability, fail altogether elsewhere. The formula is, in the mathematical phrase, a function of so many independent variables, that it must be complex beyond all conception, if it takes them all into account; while it must yet be necessarily inaccurate if it does not take them into account. But, besides this, the conditions upon which the law obviously depends are not themselves capable of being accurately defined, and still less of being numerically stated. Ingenious thinkers have, indeed, tried to apply mathematical formulæ to psychology; but they have not got very far; and it may, I think, be assumed, without further argument, that while you have to deal both with psychological and sociological elements, with human desires, and with those desires modified by social relations, it is impossible to find any data which can be mathematically stated. There is no arithmetical measure of the forces of love, or hunger, or avarice, by which (among others) the whole problem is worked out.

It seems to me, therefore, that we must accept the alternative which is only mentioned to be repudiated by Jevons, namely, that Political Economy, if not a "mathematical science," must be part of sociology. I should say that it clearly is so; for if we wish to investigate the cause of any of the phenomena concerned, and not simply to tabulate from observations, we are at once concerned with the social structure and with the underlying psychology. The mathematical methods are quite in their place when dealing with statistics. The rise and fall of prices, and so forth, can be stated precisely in figures; and, whenever we can discover some approximation to a mathematical law (as in the cases I have noticed) we may work out the results. If, for example, the price of a commodity under certain conditions bears a certain relation to its scarcity, we can discover the one fact when the other fact is given, remembering only that our conclusions are not more certain than our premises, and that the observed law depends upon unknown and most imperfectly knowable conditions. Such results, again, may be very useful in various ways, as illustrative of the way in which certain laws will work if they hold good; and, again, as testing many of our general theories. If you have argued that the price of gold or silver cannot be fixed, the fact that it has been fixed under certain conditions will of course lead to a revision of your arguments. But I cannot help thinking that it is an illusion to suppose that such methods can justify the assertion that the science as a whole is "mathematical". Nothing, indeed, is easier than to speak as if you had got a mathematical theory. Let x mean the desire for marriage and y the fear of want, then the number of marriages is a function of x and y, and I can express this by symbols as well as by ordinary words. But there is no magic about the use of symbols. Mathematical inquiries are not fruitful because symbols are used, but because the symbols represent something absolutely precise and assignable. The highest mathematical inquiries are simply ingenious methods of counting; and till you have got something precise to count, they can take you no further. I cannot help thinking that this fallacy imposes upon some modern reasoners; that they assume that they have got the data because they have put together the formulæ which would be useful if they had the data; and, in short, that you can get more out of a mill than you put into it; or, in other words, that more conclusions than really follow can be got out of premises, simply because you show what would follow if you had the required knowledge. When the attempt is made, as it seems to me to be made sometimes, to deduce economical laws from some law of human desire-as from the simple theorem that equal increments of a commodity imply diminishing amounts of utility-I should reply not only that the numerical data are vaguely defined and incapable of being accurately stated, but that the attempt must be illusory because the conclusions are not determinable from the premises. The economic laws do not follow from any simple rule about human desires, because they vary according to the varying constitution of human society; and any conclusion which you could obtain would be necessarily confined to the abstract man of whom the law is supposed to hold good. Every such method, therefore, if it could be successful, could only lead to conclusions about human desire in general, and could throw no light upon the special problems of political economy, which essentially depend upon varying industrial organisation.

I will not, however, go further. You must either, I hold, limit Political Economy to the field of statistical inquiry, or admit that, as a part of sociology, it deals with questions altogether beyond the reach of mathematics. Like physiology, it is concerned with results capable of numerical statement. The number of beats of the pulse, or the number of degrees of temperature of the body, are important data in physiological problems. They may be counted, and may give rise to mathematically expressible formulæ. But the fact does not excuse us from considering the physical conditions of the organs which are in some way correlated with these observed phenomena; and, in the case of Political Economy, we have to do with the social structure, which is dependent upon forces altogether incapable of precise numerical estimates. That, at least, is my view; and I shall apply it to illustrate one remark, which must, I think, have often occurred to us. Political Economy, that is, often appears to have a negative rather than a positive value. It is exceedingly potent-so, at least, I think-in dispersing certain popular fallacies; but it fails when we regard it as a science which can give us positive concrete "laws". The general reason is, I should say, that although its first principles may be true descriptions of facts, and any denial of them, or any inconsistent applications of them, may lead us into error, they are yet far from sufficient descriptions. They omit some considerations which are relevant in any concrete case; and the facts which they describe are so complex that, even when we look at them consistently and follow the right clue, we cannot solve the complicated problems which occur. It may be worth while to insist a little upon this, and to apply it to one or two peculiar problems.

Let me start from the ordinary analogy. Economic inquiry, I have suggested, describes a certain existing mechanism, which exists as really as the physical structure described by an anatomist. The industrial organism has, of course, many properties of which the economist, as such, does not take account. The labourer has affections, and imaginations, and opinions outside of his occupation as labourer; he belongs to a state, a church, a family, and so forth, which affect his whole life, including his industrial life. Is it therefore impossible to consider the industrial organisation separately? Not more impossible, I should reply, than to apply the same method in regard to the individual body. Were I to regard my stomach simply as a bag into which I put my food, I should learn very little about the process of digestion. Still, it is such a bag, and it is important to know where it is, and what are its purely mechanical relations to other parts of the body. My arms and legs are levers, and I can calculate the pressure necessary to support a weight on the hand, as though my bones and muscles were made of iron and whipcord. I am a piece of mechanism, though I am more, and all the principles of simple mechanics apply to my actions, though they do not, by themselves, suffice to explain the actions. The discovery of the circulation of the blood explained, as I understand, my structure as a hydraulic apparatus; and it was of vast importance, even though it told us nothing directly of the other processes necessarily involved. In this case, therefore, we have an instance of the way in which a set of perfectly true propositions may, so to speak, be imbedded in a larger theory, and may be of the highest importance, though they are not by themselves sufficient to solve any concrete problem. We cannot, that is, deduce the physiological principles from the mechanical principles, although they are throughout implied. But those principles are not the less true and useful in the detection of fallacies. They may enable us to show that an argument supposes facts which do not exist; or, perhaps, that it is, at any rate, inconsistent because it assumes one structure in its premisses, and another in its conclusions.

I state this by way of illustration: but the value of the remark may be best tested by applying it to some economical doctrines. Let us take, for example, the famous argument of Adam Smith against what he called the mercantile theory. That theory, according to him, supposed that the wealth of nations, like the wealth of an individual, was in proportion to the amount of money in their possession. He insisted upon the theory that money, as it is useful solely for exchange, cannot be, in itself, wealth; that its absolute amount is a matter of indifference, because if every coin in existence were halved or doubled, it would discharge precisely the same function; and he inferred that the doctrine which tested the advantages of foreign commerce by the balance of trade or the net return of money, was altogether illusory. His theory is expounded in every elementary treatise on the subject. It may be urged that it was a mere truism, and therefore useless; or, again, that it does not enable us to deduce a complete theory of the functions of money. In regard to the first statement, I should reply that, although Smith probably misrepresented some of his antagonists, the fallacy which he exposed was not only current at the time, but is still constantly cropping up in modern controversies. So long as arguments are put forward which implicitly involve an erroneous, because self-contradictory, conception of the true functions of money, it is essential to keep in mind these first principles, however obvious they may be in an abstract statement. Euclid's axioms are useful because they are self-evident; and so long as people make mistakes in geometry, it will be necessary to expose their blundering by bringing out the contradictions involved. As Hobbes observed, people would dispute even geometrical axioms if they had an interest in doing so; and, certainly, they are ready to dispute the plainest doctrines about money. The other remark, that we cannot deduce a complete theory from the axiom is, of course, true. Thus, for example, although the doctrine may be unimpeachable, there is a difficulty in applying it to the facts. As gold has other uses besides its use as money, its value is not regulated exclusively by the principle assigned; as other things, again, such as bank-notes and cheques, discharge some of the functions of money, we have all manner of difficult problems as to what money precisely is, and how the most elementary principles will apply to the concrete facts. A very shrewd economist once remarked, listening to a metaphysical argument, "If there had been any money to be made out of it, we should have solved that question in the city long ago". Yet, there is surely money to be made out of a correct theory of the currency; and people in the city do not seem to have arrived at a complete agreement. In fact, such controversies illustrate the extreme difficulty which arises out of the complexity of the phenomena, even where the economic assumption of the action of purely money-loving activity is most nearly verified. The moral is, I fancy, that while inaccurate conclusions are extremely difficult, we can only hope to approach them by a firm grasp of the first principles revealed in the simplest cases.

Even in such a case, we have also to notice how we have to make allowance for the intrusion of other than purely economic cases. The doctrine just noticed is, of course, closely connected with the theory of free trade. The free trade argument is, I should mention, perfectly conclusive in a negative sense. It demonstrates, that is, the fallacy which lurks in the popular argument for protection. That argument belongs to the commonest class of economic fallacies, which consists in looking at one particular result without considering the necessary implications. The great advantage of any rational theory is, that it forces us to look upon the industrial mechanism as a whole, and to trace out the correlative changes involved in any particular operation. It disposes of the theories which virtually propose to improve our supply of water by pouring a cup out of one vessel into another; and such theories have had considerable success in economy. So far, in short, as a protectionist really maintains that the advantage consists in accumulating money, without asking what will be the effect upon the value of money, or that it consists in telling people to make for themselves what they could get on better terms by producing something to exchange for it, his arguments may be conclusively shown to be contradictory. Such arguments, at least, cannot be worth considering. But, to say nothing of cases which may be put by an ingenious disputant in which this may not quite apply, we have to consider reasons which may be extra-economical. When it is suggested, for example, that the economic disadvantage is a fair price for political independence; or, on the other hand, that the stimulus of competition is actually good for the trade affected; or, again, that protection tends naturally to corruption; we have arguments which, good or bad, are outside the sphere of economics proper. To answer them we have to enter the field of political or ethical inquiry, where we have to take leave of tangible facts and precise measures.

This is a more prominent element as we approach the more human side (if I may so call it) of Political Economy. Consider, for example, the doctrine which made so profound an impression upon the old school-Malthus's theory of population. It was summed up in the famous-though admittedly inaccurate-phrase, that population had a tendency to increase in a geometrical ratio, while the means of subsistence increased only in an arithmetical ratio. The food available for each unit would therefore diminish as the population increased. The so-called law obviously states only a possibility. It describes a "tendency," or, in other words, only describes what would happen under certain, admittedly variable, conditions. It showed how, in a limited area and with the efficiency of industry remaining unaltered, the necessary limits upon the numbers of the population would come into play. If, then, the law were taken, or in so far as it was taken, to assert that, in point of fact, the population must always be increasing in civilised countries to the stage at which the lowest class would be at starvation level, it was certainly erroneous. There are cases in which statesmen are alarmed by the failure of population to show its old elasticity, and beginning to revert to the view that an increased rate is desirable. It cannot be said to be even necessarily true that in all cases an increased population implies, of necessity, increased difficulty of support. There are countries which are inadequately peopled, and where greater numbers would be able to support themselves more efficiently because they could adopt a more elaborate organisation. Nor can it be said with certainty that some pressure may not, within limits, be favourable to ultimate progress by stimulating the energies of the people. In a purely stationary state people might be too content with a certain stage of comfort to develop their resources and attain a permanently higher stage. Whatever the importance of such qualifications of the principle, there is a most important conclusion to be drawn. Malthus or his more rigid followers summed up their teaching by one practical moral. The essential condition of progress was, according to them, the discouragement of early marriages. If, they held, people could only be persuaded not to produce families until they had an adequate prospect of supporting their families, everything would go right. We shall not, I imagine, be inclined to dispute the proposition, that a certain degree of prudence and foresight is a quality of enormous value; and that such a quality will manifest itself by greater caution in taking the most important step in life. What such reasoners do not appear to have appreciated was, the immense complexity and difficulty of the demand which they were making. They seem to have fancied that it was possible simply to add another clause-the clause "Thou shalt not marry"-to the accepted code of morals; and that, as soon as the evil consequences of the condemned behaviour were understood,-properly expounded, for example, in little manuals for the use of school children,-obedience to the new regulation would spontaneously follow. What they did not see, or did not fully appreciate, was the enormous series of other things-religious, moral, and intellectual-which are necessarily implied in altering the relation of the strongest human passion to the general constitution, and the impossibility of bringing home such an alteration, either by an act of legislation or by pointing out the bearing of a particular set of prudential considerations. Political Economy might be a very good thing; but its expositors were certainly too apt to think that it could by itself at once become a new gospel for mankind. Should we then infer from such criticisms that the doctrine of Malthus was false, or was of no importance? Nothing would be further from my opinion. I hold, on the contrary, that it was of the highest importance, because it drew attention to a fact, the recognition of which was essential to all sound reasoning on social questions. The fact is, that population is not to be treated as a fixed quantity, but as capable of rapid expansion; and that this elasticity may at any moment require consideration, and does in fact give the explanation of many important phenomena. The main fact which gave importance to Malthus's writings was the rapid and enormous increase of pauperism during the first quarter of this century. The charitable and sentimental writers of the day were alarmed, but proposed to meet the evil by a reckless increase of charity, either of the official or the private variety. Pitt, we know, declared (though he qualified the statement) that to be the father of a large family should be a source of honour, not of obloquy; and the measures adopted under the influence of such notions did in fact tend to diminish all sense of responsibility, encouraged people to rely upon the parish for the support of their children, and brought about a state of things which alarmed all intelligent observers. The greatest check to the evil was given by the new Poor-law, adopted under the influence of the principles advocated by Malthus and his friends. His achievement, then, was not that he laid down any absolutely correct scientific truth, or even said anything which had not been more or less said by many judicious people before his time; but that he encouraged the application of a more systematic method of reasoning upon the great problem of the time. Instead of simply giving way to the first kindly impulse, abolishing a hardship here and distributing alms elsewhere, he substantially argued that society formed a complex organism, whose diseases should be considered physiologically, their causes explained, and the appropriate remedies considered in all their bearings. We must not ask simply whether we were giving a loaf to this or that starving man, or indulge in à priori reasoning as to the right of every human being to be supported by others; but treat the question as a physician should treat a disease, and consider whether, on the whole, the new regulations would increase or diminish the causes of the existing evils. He did not, therefore, so much proclaim a new truth, as induce reformers to place themselves at a new and a more rational point of view. The so-called law of population which he announced might be in various ways inaccurate, but the announcement made it necessary for rational thinkers to take constantly into account considerations which are essential in any satisfactory treatment of the great problems. If it were right to consider pauperism as a gulf of fixed dimensions, we might hope to fill it by simply taking a sufficient quantity of wealth from the richer classes. If, as Malthus urged, this process had a tendency to enlarge the dimensions of the gulf itself, it was obvious that the whole problem required a more elaborate treatment. By impressing people with this truth, and by showing how, in a great variety of cases, the elasticity of the population was a most important factor in determining the condition of the people, Malthus did a great service, and introduced a more systematic and scientific method of discussing the immensely important questions involved.

I will very briefly try to indicate one further application of economic principles. A critical point in the modern development of the study was marked by Mill's abandonment of the so-called "wage fund theory". That doctrine is now generally mentioned with contempt, as the most conspicuous instance of an entirely exploded theory. It is often said that it is either a falsity, or a barren truism. I am not about to argue the point, observing only that some very eminent Economists consider that it was rather inadequate than fallacious; and that to me it has always seemed that the theory which has really been confuted is not so much a theory which was ever actually held by Economists, as a formula into which they blundered when they tried to give a quasi-scientific definition of their meaning. It is common enough for people to argue sensibly, when the explicit statements of their argument may be altogether erroneous. At any rate, I think it has been a misfortune that a good phrase has been discredited; and that Mill's assailants, in exposing the errors of that particular theory of a "wage fund," seemed to imply that the whole conception of a "wage fund" was a mistake. For the result has been, that the popular mind seems to regard the amount spent in wages as an arbitrary quantity; as something which, as Malthus put it, might be fixed at pleasure by her Majesty's justices of the peace. Because the law was inaccurately stated, it is assumed that there is no law at all, and that the share of the labourers in the total product of industry might be fixed without reference to the effect of a change upon the general organisation. Now, if the wage fund means the share which, under existing circumstances, actually goes to the class dependent upon wages, it is of the highest importance to discover how that share is actually determined; and it does not even follow that a doctrine which is in some sense a truism may not be a highly important doctrine. One of the ablest of the old Economists, Nassau Senior, after laying down his version of the theory, observes that it is "so nearly self-evident" that if Political Economy were a new science, it might be taken for granted. But he proceeds to enumerate seven different opinions, some of them held by many people, and others by writers of authority, with which it is inconsistent. And, without following his arguments, this statement suggests what I take to be a really relevant defence of his reasons. At the time when the theory was first formulated, there were many current doctrines which were self-contradictory, and which could, therefore, best be met by the assertion of a truism. When the peace of 815 brought distress instead of plenty, some people, such as Southey, thought it a sufficient explanation to say that the manufacturer had lost his best customer, because the Government wanted fewer guns and less powder. They chose to overlook the obvious fact that a customer who pays for his goods by taking money out of the pockets of the seller, is not an unmixed blessing. Then, there was the theory of general "gluts," and of what is still denounced as over-production. The best cure for commercial distress would be, as one disputant asserted, to burn all the goods in our warehouses. It was necessary to point out that this theory (when stated in superficial terms) regarded superabundance of wealth as the cause of universal poverty. Another common theory was the evil effect of manufacturers in displacing work. The excellent Robert Owen stated it as an appalling fact, that the cotton manufacture supplanted the labour of a hundred (perhaps it was two hundred) millions of men. He seems to assume that, if the machinery had not been there, there would still have been wages for the hundred millions. The curious confusion, indeed, which leads us to speak of men wanting work, when what we really mean is that they want wages, shows the tenacity of an old fallacy. Mandeville argued long ago that the fire of London was a blessing, because it set at work so many carpenters, plumbers, and glaziers. The Protestant Reformation had done less good than the invention of hooped petticoats, which had provided employment for so many milliners. I shall not insult you by exposing fallacies; and yet, so long as they survive, they have to be met by truisms. While people are proposing to lengthen their blankets by cutting off one end to sew upon the other, one has to point out that the total length remains constant. Now, I fancy that, in point of fact, these fallacies are often to be found in modern times. I read, the other day, in the papers, an argument, adduced by some advocate, on behalf of the Eight Hours Bill. He wished, he said, to make labour dear, and would therefore make it scarce. This apparently leads to the conclusion that the less people work the more they will get, which I take to be a fallacy. So, to mention nothing else, it is still apparently a common argument in favour of protection in America, that the native labourer requires to be supported against the pauperised labour of Europe. Americans in general are to be made richer by paying higher prices, and by being forced to produce commodities which they could get with less labour employed on the production of other things in exchange. I will not go further; for I think that no one who reads the common arguments can be in want of sufficient illustrations of popular fallacies. This, I say, is some justification for dwelling upon the contrary truisms. I admit, indeed, that even these fallacies may apply to particular cases in which they may represent partial truths; and I also agree that, as sometimes stated, the wage fund theory was not only a truism, but a fruitless truism. It was, however, as I believe, an attempt to generalise a very pertinent and important doctrine, as to the way in which the actual competition in which labourers and employers are involved, actually operates. If so, it requires rather modification than indiscriminate denunciation; and it is, I believe, so treated by the best modern Economists. I consider, then, that the Economists were virtually attempting to describe systematically the main relations of the industrial mechanism. They showed what were the main functions which it, in fact, discharges. Their theory was sufficient to expose many errors, especially those which arise from looking solely at one part of a complex process, and neglecting the implied reactions. It enabled them to point out the inconsistencies and actual contradictions involved in many popular arguments, which are still very far from being destroyed. Their main error-apart from any particular logical slips-was, namely, that when they had laid down certain principles which belong properly to the prolegomena of the science, and which are very useful when regarded as providing logical tests of valid reasoning, they imagined that they had done a great deal more, and that the desired science was actually constituted. They laid down three or four primary axioms, such as the doctrine that men desire wealth, and fancied that the whole theory could be deduced from them. This, if what I have said be true, was really to misunderstand what they were really doing. It was to suppose that you could obtain a description of social phenomena without examining the actual structure of society; and was as erroneous as to suppose that you could deduce physiological truths from a few general propositions about the mechanical relations of the skeleton. Such criticisms have been made by the historical school of Economists; and I, at least, can fully accept their general view. I quite agree that the old assumptions of the older school were frequently unjustifiable; nor can I deny that they laid them down with a tone of superlative dogmatism, which was apt to be very offensive, and which was not justified by their position. Moreover, I entirely agree that the progress of economic science, and of all other moral sciences, requires a historical basis; and that we should make a very great blunder if we thought that the creation of an economic man would justify us in dispensing with an investigation of concrete facts, both of the present day and of earlier stages of industrial evolution. But to this there is an obvious qualification. What do we mean by investigating facts? It seems to be a very simple rule, but it leads us at once to great difficulties. So, as Mill and later writers have very rightly asked, how are we to settle even the most obvious questions in inquiries where, for obvious reasons, we cannot make experiments, and where we have not such a set of facts as would spontaneously give us the truths which we might seek by experiment? Take, as Mill suggested, such a question as free trade. We cannot get two countries alike in all else, and differing only in respect to their adoption or rejection of a protective tariff. Anything like a thoroughgoing system of free trade has been tried in England alone; and the commercial prosperity of the country since its adoption has been affected by innumerable conditions, so that it is altogether impossible to isolate the results which are to be attributed to the negative condition of the absence of protection. Briefly, the result is that the phenomena with which we have to deal are so complex, and our power of arranging them so as to unravel the complexity is so limited, that the direct method of observation breaks down altogether. Mill confessed the necessity of applying a different method, which he described with great ability, and which substantially amounts to the method of the older Economists. If, with some writers of the historical school, we admit the objections which apply to this method, we seem to be reduced to a hopeless state of uncertainty. A treatise on Political Economy becomes nothing but a miscellaneous collection of facts, with no definite clue or uniform method of reasoning. I must beg, in conclusion, to indicate what, so far as I can guess, seems to be the view suggested in presence of this difficulty.

If I am asked whether Political Economy, understood, for example, as Mill understood it, is to be regarded as a science, I should have to admit that I could not simply reply, Yes. To say nothing of any errors in his logic, I should say that I do not believe that it gives us sufficient guidance even in regard to economic phenomena. We could not, that is, deduce from the laws accepted by Economists the necessary working of any given measure-say, the effect of protection or free trade, or, still more, the making of a poor-law system. Such problems involve elements of which the Economist, purely as an Economist, is an incompetent judge; and the further we get from those questions in which purely economical considerations are dominant, towards those in which other factors become relevant,-from questions as to currency, for example, to questions as to the relations of capitalists and labourers,-the greater the inadequacy of our methods. But I also hold that Political Economists may rightly claim a certain scientific character for their speculations. If their ultimate aim is to frame a science of economics which shall be part of the science-not yet constituted-of sociology, then I should say that what they have really done-so far as they have reasoned accurately-has been to frame an essential part of the prolegomena to such a science. The "laws" which they have tried to formulate are not laws which, even if established, would enable us to predict the results of any given action; but they are laws which would have to be taken into account in attempting any such prediction. And this is so, I think, because the laws are descriptions-within limits accurate descriptions-of actually existing facts as to the social mechanism. They are not mere abstract hypotheses, in the sense sometimes attached to that phrase; but accounts of the plan upon which the industrial arrangements of civilised countries are, as a matter of fact, constructed. Such a classification and systematic account of facts is, as I should suggest, absolutely necessary for any sound historical method. Facts are not simply things lying about, which anybody can pick up and describe for the mere pains of collecting them. We cannot even see a fact without reflection and observation and judgment; and to arrange them in an order which shall be both systematic and fruitful, to look at them from that point of view in which we can detect the general underlying principles, is, in all cases, an essential process before we can begin to apply a truly historical method. Anything, it is said, may be proved by facts; and that is painfully true until we have the right method of what has been called "colligating" facts. The Catholic and the Protestant, the Conservative and the Radical, the Individualist and the Socialist, have equal facility in proving their own doctrines with arguments, which habitually begin, "All history shows". Printers should be instructed always to strike out that phrase as an erratum; and to substitute, "I choose to take for granted". In order to judge between them we have to come to some conclusion as to what is the right method of conceiving of history, and probably to try many methods before reaching that which arranges the shifting and complicated chaos of phenomena in something like an intelligible order. A first step and a necessary basis, as I believe, for all the more complex inquiries will have to be found by disentangling the various orders of laws (if I may so speak), and considering by themselves those laws of industrial growth which are nearest to the physical sciences in certain respects, and which, within certain limits, can be considered apart, inasmuch as they represent the working of forces which are comparatively independent of forces of a higher order. What I should say for Political Economists is that they have done a good deal in this direction; that they have explained, and, I suppose, with considerable accuracy, what is the actual nature of the industrial mechanism; that they have explained fairly its working in certain cases where the economic are practically also the sole or dominant motives; and that they have thus laid down certain truths which require attention even when we take into account the play of other more complex and, as we generally say, higher motives. We may indeed hope and believe that society will ultimately be constituted upon a different system; and that for the organisation which has spontaneously and unconsciously developed itself, another will be substituted which will correspond more closely to some principles of justice, and give freer scope for the full development of the human faculties. That is a very large question: I only say that, in any case, all genuine progress consists in a development of institutions already existing, and therefore that a full understanding of the working of the present system is essential to a rational consideration of possible improvements. The Socialist may look forward to a time-let us hope that it may come soon!-when nobody will have any grievances. But his schemes will be the better adapted for the realisation of his hopes in proportion as he has fully understood what is the part played by each factor of the existing system; what is its function, and how that function may be more efficiently discharged by any substitute. Only upon that condition can he avoid the common error of inventing some scheme which is in sociology what schemes for perpetual motion are in mechanics; plans for making everything go right by condemning some existing portion of the system without fully understanding how it has come into existence, and what is the part which it plays in the whole. I think myself that a study of the good old orthodox system of Political Economy is useful in this sense, even where it is wrong; because at least it does give a system, and therefore forces its opponents to present an alternative system, instead of simply cutting a hole in the shoe when it pinches, or striking out the driving wheel because it happens to creak unpleasantly. And I think so the more because I cannot but observe that whenever a real economic question presents itself, it has to be argued on pretty much the old principles, unless we take the heroic method of discarding argument altogether. I should be the last to deny that the old Political Economy requires careful revision and modification, and equally slow to deny that the limits of its applicability require to be carefully defined. But, with these qualifications, I say, with equal conviction, that it does lay down principles which require study and consideration, for the simple reason that they assert the existence of facts which are relevant and important in all the most vitally interesting problems of to-day.

THE MORALITY OF COMPETITION

When it has occurred to me to say-as I have occasionally said-that, to my mind, the whole truth lies neither with the individualist nor with his antagonist, my friends have often assured me that I was illogical. Of two contradictory principles, they say, you must take one. There are cases, I admit, in which this remark applies. It is true, or it is not true, that two and two make four. We cannot, in arithmetic, adopt Sir Roger de Coverley's conciliatory view, that there is much to be said on both sides. But this logical rule supposes that, in point of fact, the two principles apply to the same case, and are mutually exclusive. I also think that the habit of taking for granted that social problems are reducible to such an alternative, is the source of innumerable fallacies. I hold that, as a rule, any absolute solution of such problems is impossible; and that a man who boasts of being logical, is generally announcing his deliberate intention to be one-sided. He is confusing the undeniable canon that of two contradictory propositions one must be true, with the assumption that two propositions are really contradictory. The apparent contradiction may be illusory. Society, says the individualist, is made up of all its members. Certainly: if all Englishmen died, there would be no English race. But it does not follow that every individual Englishman is not also the product of the race. Society, says the Socialist, is an organic whole. I quite admit the fact; but it does not follow that, as a whole, it has any qualities or aims independent of the qualities and aims of the constituent parts. Metaphysicians have amused themselves, in all ages, with the puzzle about the many and the one. Perhaps they may find contradictions in the statement that a human society is both one and many; a unit and yet complex; but I am content to assume that unless we admit the fact, we shall get a very little way in sociology.

Society, we say, is an organism. That implies that every part of a society is dependent upon the other parts, and that although, for purposes of argument, we may find it convenient to assume that certain elements remain fixed while others vary, we must always remember that this is an assumption which, in the long run, never precisely corresponds to the facts. We may, for example, in economical questions, attend simply to the play of the ordinary industrial machinery, without taking into account the fact that the industrial machinery is conditioned by the political and ecclesiastical constitution, by the whole social order, and, therefore, by the acceptance of corresponding ethical, or philosophical or scientific creeds. The method is justifiable so long as we remember that we are using a logical artifice; but we blunder if we take our hypothesis for a full statement of the actual facts. We are then tempted, and it is, perhaps, the commonest of all sources of error in such inquiries, to assume that conditions are absolute which are really contingent; or, to attend only to the action, without noticing the inevitable reactions of the whole system of institutions. And I would suggest, that from this follows a very important lesson in such inquiries. To say that this or that part of a system is bad, is to say, by implication, that some better arrangement is possible consistently with our primary assumptions. In other words, we cannot rationally propose simply to cut out one part of a machine, dead or living, without considering the effect of the omission upon all the other dependent parts. The whole system is necessarily altered. What, we must therefore ask, is the tacit implication as well as what is the immediate purpose of a change? May not the bad effect be a necessary part of the system to which we also owe the good; or necessary under some conditions? It is always, therefore, a relevant question, what is the suggested alternative? We can then judge whether the removal of a particular evil is or is not to be produced at a greater cost than it is worth; whether it would be a process, say, of really curing a smoky chimney or of stopping the chimney altogether, and so abolishing not only the smoke but the fire.

I propose to apply this to the question of "competition". Competition is frequently denounced as the source of social evils. The complaint is far from a new one. I might take for my text a passage from J. S. Mill's famous chapter on the probable future of the labouring classes. Mill, after saying that he agrees with the Socialists in their practical aims, declares his utter dissent from their declamations against competition. "They forget," he says, "that where competition is not, monopoly is; and that monopoly, in all its forms, is the taxation of the industrious for the support of indolence, if not of plunder." That suggests my question: If competition is bad, what is good? What is the alternative to competition? Is it, as Mill says, monopoly, or is any third choice possible? If it is monopoly, do you defend monopoly, or only monopoly in some special cases? I opened, not long ago, an old book of caricatures, in which the revolutionary leader is carrying a banner with the double inscription, "No monopoly! No competition!" The implied challenge-how can you abolish both?-seemed to me to require a plain answer. Directly afterwards I then took up the newspaper, and read the report of an address upon the prize-day of a school. The speaker dwelt in the usual terms upon the remorseless and crushing competition of the present day, which he mentioned as an incitement to every boy to get a good training for the struggle. The moral was excellent; but it seemed to me curious that the speaker should be denouncing competition in the very same breath with proofs of its influence in encouraging education. When I was a lad, a clever boy and a stupid boy had an equal chance of getting an appointment to a public office. The merit which won a place might be relationship to a public official, or perhaps to a gentleman who had an influence in the constituency of the official. The system was a partial survival of the good old days in which, according to Sam Weller, the young nobleman got a position because his mother's uncle's wife's grandfather had once lighted the King's pipe. The nobleman, I need hardly add, considered this as an illustration of the pleasant belief, "Whatever is, is right". As we had ceased to accept that opinion in politics, offices were soon afterwards thrown open to competition, with the general impression that we were doing justice and opening a career to merit. That the resulting system has grave defects is, I think, quite undeniable; but so far as it has succeeded in determining that the men should be selected for public duty, for their fitness, and for nothing else, it is surely a step in advance which no one would now propose to retrace. And yet it was simply a substitution of competition for monopoly. As it comes into wider operation, some of us begin to cry out against competition. The respectable citizen asks, What are we to do with our boys? The obvious reply is, that he really means, What are we to do with our fools? A clever lad can now get on by his cleverness; and of course those who are not clever are thrust aside. That is a misfortune, perhaps, for them; but we can hardly regard it as a misfortune for the country. And clearly, too, pressure of this kind is likely to increase. We have come to believe that it is a main duty of the nation to provide general education. When the excellent Miss Hannah More began to spread village schools, she protested warmly that she would not teach children anything which would tend to make the poor discontented with their station. They must learn to read the Bible, but she hoped that they would stop short of such knowledge as would enable them to read Tom Paine. Now, Hannah More deserves our gratitude for her share in setting the ball rolling; but it has rolled far beyond the limits she would have prescribed. We now desire not only that every child in the country should be able to acquire the elements of learning at least; but, further, we hope that ladders may be provided by which every promising child may be able to climb beyond the elements, and to acquire the fullest culture of which his faculties are capable. There is not only no credit at the present day in wishing so much, but it is discreditable not to do what lies in one's power to further its accomplishment. But, then, is not that to increase enormously the field of competition? I, for example, am a literary person, after a fashion; I have, that is, done something to earn a living by my pen. I had the advantage at starting of belonging to the small class which was well enough off to send its children to the best schools and universities. That is to say, I was one of the minority which had virtually a monopoly of education, and but for that circumstance I should in all probability have taken to some possibly more honest, but perhaps even worse paid, occupation. Every extension of the margin of education, everything which diffuses knowledge and intellectual training through a wider circle, must increase the competition among authors. If every man with brains, whether born in a palace or a cottage is to have a chance of making the best of them, the capacity for authorship, and therefore the number of competitors, will be enormously spread. It may also, we will hope, increase the demand for their work. The same remark applies to every profession for which intellectual culture is a qualification. Do we regret the fact? Would we sentence three-quarters of the nation to remain stupid, in order that the fools in the remaining quarter may have a better chance? That would be contrary to every democratic instinct, to the highest as well as the lowest. But if I say, every office and every profession shall be open to every man; success in it shall depend upon his abilities and merits; and, further, every child in the country shall have the opportunity of acquiring the necessary qualifications, what is that but to accept and to stimulate the spirit of competition? What, I ask, is the alternative? Should people be appointed by interest? Or is nobody to be anxious for official or professional or literary or commercial success, but only to develop his powers from a sense of duty, and wait till some infallible observer comes round and says, "Friend, take this position, which you deserve"? Somehow I do not think that last scheme practicable at present. But, even in that case, I do not see how the merits of any man are to be tested without enabling him to prove by experiment that he is the most meritorious person; and, if that be admitted, is not every step in promoting education, in equalising, therefore, the position from which men start for the race, a direct encouragement to competition?

Carlyle was fond of saying that Napoleon's great message to mankind was the declaration that careers should be open to talent, or the tools given to him who could use them. Surely that was a sound principle; and one which, so far as I can see, cannot be applied without stimulating competition. The doctrine, indeed, is unpalatable to many Socialists. To me, it seems to be one to which only the cowardly and the indolent can object in principle. Will not a society be the better off, in which every man is set to work upon the tasks for which he is most fitted? If we allowed our teaching and our thinking to be done by blockheads; our hard labour to be done by men whose muscles were less developed than their brains; made our soldiers out of our cowards, and our sailors out of the sea-sick,-should we be better off? It seems, certainly, to me, that whatever may be the best constitution of society, one mark of it will be the tendency to distribute all social functions according to the fitness of the agents; to place trust where trust is justifiable, and to give the fullest scope for every proved ability, intellectual, moral, and physical. Of course, such approximation to this result, as we can observe in the present order of things, is very imperfect. Many of the most obvious evils in the particular system of competition now adopted, may be summed up in the statement, that the tests according to which success is awarded, are not so contrived as to secure the success of the best competitors. Some of them, for example, are calculated to give an advantage to the superficial and the showy. But that is to say that they are incompatible with the true principle which they were intended to embody; and that we should reform our method, not in the direction of limiting competition, but in the direction of so framing our system that it may be a genuine application of Carlyle's doctrine. In other words, in all the professions for which intellectual excellence is required, the conditions should be such as to give the best man the best chance, as far as human arrangements can secure that object. What other rule can be suggested? Competition, in this sense, means the preservation of the very atmosphere which is necessary to health; and to denounce it is either to confirm the most selfish and retrograde principles, or to denounce something which is only called competition by a confusion of ideas. How easy such a confusion may be, is obvious when we look at the ordinary language about industrial competition. We are told that wages are kept down by competition. To this Mill replied in the passage I have quoted, and, upon his own theory, at any rate, replied with perfect justice, that they were also kept up by competition. The common language upon the subject is merely one instance of the fallacies into which men fall when they personify an abstraction. Competition becomes a kind of malevolent and supernatural being, to whose powers no conceivable limits are assigned. It is supposed to account for any amount of degradation. Yet if, by multiplying their numbers, workmen increase supply, and so lower the price of labour, it follows, conversely, by the very same reasoning, that if they refused to multiply, they would diminish the supply and raise the price. The force, by its very nature, operates as certainly in one direction as in the other. If, again, there is competition among workmen, there is competition among capitalists. In every strike, of course, workmen apply the principle, and sometimes apply it very effectually, in the attempt to raise their wages. It was often argued, indeed, that in this struggle, the employer possessed advantages partly due to his power of forming tacit combinations. The farmers in a parish, or the manufacturers in a business, were pledged to each other not to raise the rate of wages. If that be so, you again complain, not of competition, but of the want of competition; and you agree that the labourer will benefit, as in fact, I take it, he has undoubtedly benefited, by freer competition among capitalists, or by the greater power of removing his own labour to better markets. In such cases, the very meaning of the complaint is not that there is competition, but that the competition is so arranged as to give an unfair advantage to one side. And a similar misunderstanding is obviously implied in other cases. The Australian or American workman fears that his wages will be lowered by the competition of the Chinese; and the Englishman protests against the competition of pauper aliens. Let us assume that he is right in believing that such competition will tend to lower his wages, whatever the moral to be drawn from the fact. Briefly, denunciations of "competition" in this sense are really complaints that we do not exclude the Chinese immigrant and therefore give a monopoly to the native labourer. That may be a good thing for him, and if it be not a good thing for the Chinaman who is excluded from the field, we perhaps do not care very much about the results to China. We are so much better than the heathen that we need not bother about their interests. But, of course, the English workman, when he complains of the intensity of competition, does not propose to adopt the analogous remedy of giving a monopoly to one section of our own population. The English pauper is here; we do not want to suppress him, but only to suppress his pauperism; and he certainly cannot be excluded from any share in the fund devoted to the support of labour. The evil, therefore, of which we complain is primarily the inadequacy of the support provided, not,-though that may also be complained of,-the undesirable method by which those funds are distributed. In other words, the complaint may so far be taken to mean that there are too many competitors, not that, given the competitors, their shares are determined by competition, instead of being determined by monopoly or by some other principle.

We have therefore to inquire whether any principle can be suggested which will effect the desired end, and which will yet really exclude competition. The popular suggestion is that the remedy lies in suppressing competition by equalising the prizes. If no prizes are to be won, there will so far be less reason for competing. Enough may be provided for all by simply taking something from those who have too much. Now, I may probably assume that we all agree in approving the contemplated end-a greater equality of wealth, and especially an elevation of the lower classes to a higher position in the scale of comfort. Every social reformer, whatever his particular creed, would probably agree that some of us are too rich, and that a great many are too poor. But we still have to ask, in what sense it is conceivable that a real suppression of competition can contribute to the desired end. It is obvious that when we denounce competition we often mean not that it is to be abolished, but that it is to be regulated and limited in its application. So, for example, people sometimes speak as if competition were the antithesis to co-operation. But I need hardly say that individualists, as well as their opponents, may legitimately sing the praises of co-operation. Nobody was more forward than Mill, for example, and Mill's followers, in advocating the principles of the early co-operative societies. He and they rejoiced to believe that the co-operative societies had revealed unsuspected virtues and capacities in the class from which they sprang; that they had done much to raise the standard of life and to extend sympathy and human relations among previously disconnected units of society. But it is, of course, equally obvious that they have grown up in a society which supposes free competition in every part of its industrial system; that co-operative societies, so far as the outside world is concerned, have to buy in the cheapest and sell in the dearest market; that the rate of wages of their members is still fixed by competition; and that they encourage habits of saving and forethought which presuppose that each man is to have private ends of his own. In what sense, then, can co-operation ever be regarded as really opposed to competition? Competition may exist among groups of men just as much as among individuals: a state of war is not less a state of war if it is carried on by regiments and armies, instead of by mere chaotic struggles in which each man fights for his own hand. Competition does not mean that there should be no combination, but that there should be no monopoly. So long as a trade or a profession is open to every one who chooses to take it up, its conduct will be equally regulated by competition, whether it be competition as between societies or individuals, or whether its profits be divided upon one system or another between the various classes concerned. Co-operators, of course, may look forward to a day in which society at large will be members of a single co-operative society; or, again, to a time in which every industrial enterprise may be conducted by the State. Supposing any such aspiration to be realised, the question still remains, whether they would amount to the abolition or still only to the shifting of the incidence of competition. Socialists tell us that hitherto the labourer has not had his fair share of the produce of industry. The existing system has sanctioned a complicated chicanery, by which one class has been enabled to live as mere bloodsuckers and parasites upon the rest of society. Property is the result of theft, instead of being, as Economists used to assure us, the reward of thrift. It is hoped that these evils may be remedied by a reconstruction of society, in which the means of production shall all be public property, and every man's income be simply a salary in proportion to the quantity of his labour. If we, then, ask how far competition would be abolished, we may first make one remark. Such a system, like every other system, requires, for its successful working, that the instincts and moral impulses should correspond to the demands of the society. Absolute equality of property is just as compatible with universal misery as with universal prosperity. A population made up of thoroughly lazy, sensual, stupid individuals could, if it chose, work such a machinery so as to suppress all who were industrious, refined and intelligent. However great may be the revenue of a nation, it is a very simple problem of arithmetic to discover how many people could be supported just above the starvation level. The nation at large would, on the supposed system, have to decide how its numbers and wants are to be proportioned to its means. If individuals do not compete, the whole society has, presumably, to compete with other societies; and, in every case whatever, with the general forces of nature. An indolent and inefficient majority might decide, if it pleased, that the amount of work to be exacted should be that which would be just enough to provide the simplest material necessities. If, again, the indolent and inefficient are to exist at all,-and we can scarcely count upon their disappearance,-and if further, they are to share equally with the industrious and the efficient, we must, in some way, coerce them into the required activity. If every industrial organisation is to be worked by the State, the State, it would seem, must appeal to the only means at its disposal,-namely, the prison and the scourge. If, moreover, the idle and sensual choose to multiply, the State must force them to refrain, or the standard of existence will be lowered. And, therefore, as is often argued, Socialism logically carried out would, under such conditions, lead to slavery; to a state in which labour would be enforced, and the whole system of life absolutely regulated by the will of the majority; and, in the last resort, by physical force. That seems, I confess, to be a necessary result, unless you can assume a moral change, which is entirely different from the mere change of machinery, and not necessarily implied, nor even made probable, by the change. The intellectual leaders of Socialism, no doubt, assume that the removal of "injustice" will lead to the development of a public spirit which will cause the total efficiency to be as great as it is at present, or perhaps greater. But the mass who call themselves Socialists take, one suspects, a much simpler view. They are moved by the very natural, but not especially lofty, desire to have more wages and less work. They take for granted that if their share of the total product is increased, they will get a larger dividend; and do not stop to inquire whether the advantage may be not more than counterbalanced by the diminution of the whole product, when the present incitements to industry are removed. They argue,-that is, so far as they argue at all,-as though the quantity to be distributed were a fixed quantity, and regard capitalists as pernicious persons, somehow intercepting a lion's share of the stream of wealth which, it is assumed, would flow equally if they were abolished. That is, of course, to beg the whole question.

I, however, shall venture to assume that the industrial machinery requires a corresponding moral force to work it; and I, therefore, proceed to ask how such a force can be supposed to act without some form of competition. Nothing, as a recent writer suggests,-ironically, perhaps,-could be easier than to secure an abolition of competition. You have only to do two things: to draw a "ring-fence" round your society, and then to proportion the members within the fence to the supplies. The remark suggests the difficulty. A ring-fence, for example, round London or Manchester would mean the starvation of millions in a month; or, if round England, the ruin of English commerce, the enormous rise in the cost of the poor man's food, and the abolition of all his little luxuries. But, if you include even a population as large as London, what you have next to do is to drill some millions of people-vast numbers of them poor, reckless, ignorant, sensual, and selfish-to regulate their whole mode of life by a given code, and refrain from all the pleasures which they most appreciate. The task is a big one, and not the less if you have also to undertake that everybody, whatever his personal qualities, shall have enough to lead a comfortable life. I do not suppose, however, that any rational Socialist would accept that programme of isolation. He would hold that, in his Utopia, we can do more efficiently all that is done under a system which he regards as wasteful and unjust. The existing machinery, whatever else may be said of it, does, in fact, tend to weld the whole world more and more into a single industrial organism. English workmen are labouring to satisfy the wants of other human beings in every quarter of the world; while Chinese, and Africans, and Europeans, and Americans are also labouring to satisfy theirs. This vast and almost inconceivably complex machinery has grown up in the main unconsciously, or, at least, with a very imperfect anticipation of the ultimate results, by the independent efforts of innumerable inventors, and speculators, and merchants, and manufacturers, each of them intent, as a rule, only upon his own immediate profits and the interests of the little circle with which he is in immediate contact. The theory is not, I suppose, that this gigantic system of mutual interdependence should be abolished or restricted, but that it should be carried on consciously, with definite and intelligible purpose, and in such a way as to promote the interests of every fraction of society. The whole organism should resemble one worked by a single brain, instead of representing the resultant of a multitude of distracted and conflicting forces. The difficulties are obvious enough, nor need I dwell upon them here. I will not inquire whether it does not suppose something like omniscience in the new industrial leaders; and whether the restless and multifarious energy now displayed in discovering new means of satisfying human wants could be supplied by a central body, or a number of central bodies, made up of human beings, and, moreover, official human beings, reluctant to try experiments and strike into new courses, and without the present motives for enterprise, "Individualists" have enlarged sufficiently upon such topics. What I have to note is that, in any case, the change supposes the necessity of a corresponding morality in the growth of the instincts, the public spirit, the hatred of indolence, the temperance and self-command which would be requisite to work it efficiently. The organisation into which we are born presupposes certain moral instincts, and, moreover, necessarily implies a vast system of moral discipline. Our hopes and aspirations, our judgments of our neighbours and of ourselves, are at every moment guided and moulded by the great structure of which we form a part. Whenever we ask how our lives are to be directed, what are to be the terms on which we form our most intimate ties, whom we are to support or suppress, how we are to win respect or incur contempt, we are profoundly affected by the social relations in which we are placed at our birth, and the corresponding beliefs or prejudices which we have unconsciously imbibed. Such influences, it may perhaps be said, are of incomparably greater importance than the direct exhortations to which we listen, or than the abstract doctrines which we accept in words, but which receive their whole colouring from the concrete facts to which they conform. Now, I ask how such discipline can be conceived without some kind of competition; or, rather, what would be the discipline which would remain if, in some sense, competition could be suppressed? If in the ideal society there are still prizes to be won, positions which may be the object of legitimate desire, and if those positions are to be open to every one, whatever his circumstances, we might still have the keenest competition, though carried on by different methods. If, on the other hand, no man's position were to be better than another's, we might suppress competition at the price of suppressing every motive for social as well as individual improvement. In any conceivable state of things, the welfare of every society, the total means of enjoyment at its disposal, must depend upon the energy, intelligence, and trustworthiness of its constituent members. Such qualities, I need hardly say, are qualities of individuals. Unless John and Peter and Thomas are steady, industrious, sober, and honest, the society as a whole will be neither honest nor sober nor prosperous. The problem, then, becomes, how can you ensure the existence of such qualities unless John and Peter and the rest have some advantage in virtue of possessing them? Somehow or other, a man must be the better off for doing his work well and treating his neighbour fairly. He ought surely to hold the positions in which such qualities are most required, and to have, if possible, the best chance of being a progenitor of the rising generation. A social condition in which it made no difference to a man, except so far as his own conscience was concerned, whether he were or were not honest, would imply a society favourable to people without a conscience, because giving full play to the forces which make for corruption and disintegration. If you remove the rewards accessible to the virtuous and peaceful, how are you to keep the penalties which restrain the vicious and improvident? A bare repeal of the law, "If a man will not work, neither shall he eat," would not of itself promote industry. You would at most remove the compulsion which arises from competition, to introduce the compulsion which uses physical force. You would get rid of what seems to some people the "natural" penalty of want following waste, and be forced to introduce the "artificial" or legislative penalty of compulsory labour. But, otherwise, you must construct your society so that, by the spontaneous play of society, the purer elements may rise to the surface, and the scum sink to the bottom. So long as human nature varies indefinitely, so long as we have knaves and honest men, sinners and saints, cowards and heroes, some process of energetic and active sifting is surely essential to the preservation of social health; and it is difficult to see how that is conceivable without some process of active and keen competition.

The Socialist will, of course, say, and say with too much truth, that the present form of competition is favourable to anti-social qualities. If, indeed, a capitalist is not a person who increases the productive powers of industry, but a person who manages simply to intercept a share produced by the industry of others, there is, of course, much to be said for this view. I cannot now consider that point, for my subject to-day is the moral aspect of competition considered generally. And what I have just said suggests what is, I think, the more purely moral aspect of the question. A reasonable Socialist desires to maintain what is good in the existing system, while suppressing its abuses. The question, What is good? is partly economical; but it is partly also ethical: and it is with that part that I am at present concerned.

Any system of competition, any system which supposes a reward for virtue other than virtue itself, may be accused of promoting selfishness and other ugly qualities. The doctrine that virtue is its own reward is very charming in the mouth of the virtuous man; but when his neighbours use it as an excuse for not rewarding him, it becomes rather less attractive. It saves a great deal of trouble, no doubt, and relieves us from an awkward responsibility. I must, however, point out, in the first place, that a fallacy is often introduced into these discussions which Mr. Herbert Spencer has done a great deal to expose. He has dwelt very forcibly, for example, on the fact that it is a duty to be happy and healthy; and that selfishness, if used in a bad sense, should not mean simply regard for ourselves, but only disregard for our neighbours. We ought not, in other words, to be unjust because we ourselves happen to be the objects of injustice. The parable of the good Samaritan is generally regarded as a perfect embodiment of a great moral truth. Translated from poetry into an abstract logical form, it amounts to saying that we should do good to the man who most needs our services, whatever be the accidents which alienate ordinary sympathies. Now, suppose that the good Samaritan had himself fallen among thieves, what would have been his duty? His first duty, I should say, would have been, if possible, to knock down the thief; his second, to tie up his own wounds; and his third, to call in the police. We should not, perhaps, call him virtuous for such conduct; but we should clearly think him wrong for omitting it. Not to resist a thief is cowardly; not to attend to your own health is to incapacitate yourself for duty; not to apply to the police is to be wanting in public spirit. Assuming robbery to be wrong, I am not the less bound to suppress it because I happen to be the person robbed; I am only bound not to be vindictive-that is, not to allow my personal feelings to make me act otherwise than I should act if I had no special interest in the particular case. Adam Smith's favourite rule of the "indifferent spectator" is the proper one in the case. I should be impartial, and incline no more to severity than to lenity, because I am forced by circumstances to act both as judge and as plaintiff. So, in questions of self-support, it is obviously a fallacy to assume that an action, directed in the first instance to a man's own benefit, is therefore to be stigmatised as selfish. On the good Samaritan's principle, a person should be supported, ceteris paribus, by the person who can do it most efficiently, and in nine cases out of ten that person is himself. If self-support is selfish in the sense that the service is directly rendered to self, it is not the less unselfish in so far as it is necessarily also a service to others. If I keep myself by my labour, I am preventing a burden from falling upon my fellows. And, of course, the case is stronger when I include my family. We were all impressed the other day by the story of the poor boy who got some wretchedly small pittance by his work, spent a small portion of it upon his own needs, and devoted the chief part of it to trying to save his mother and her other children from starvation. Was he selfish? Was he selfish even in taking something for himself, as the only prop of his family? What may be the immediate motive of a man when he is working for his own bread and the bread of his family may often be a difficult question; but as, in point of fact, he is helping not only himself and those who depend on him, but also in some degree relieving others from a burden, his conduct must clearly not be set down as selfish in any sense which involves moral disapproval.

Let us apply this to the case of competition. The word is generally used to convey a suggestion of selfishness in a bad sense. We think of the hardship upon the man who is ousted, as much as of the benefit to the man who gets in; or perhaps we think of it more. It suggests to us that one man has been shut out for the benefit of his neighbour; and that, of course, suggests envy, malice, and all uncharitableness. We hold that such competition must generate ill-will. I used-when I was intimately connected with a competitive system at the university-to hear occasionally of the evil influences of competition, as tending to promote jealousy between competitors. I always replied that, so far as my experience went, the evil was altogether imaginary. So far from competition generating ill-will, the keenest competitors were, as a rule, the closest friends. There was no stronger bond than the bond of rivalry in our intellectual contests. One main reason was, of course, that we had absolute faith in the fairness of the competition. We felt that it would be unworthy to complain of being beaten by a better man; and we had no doubt that, in point of fact, the winners were the better men; or, at any rate, were honestly believed to be the better men by those who distributed honours. The case, though on a small scale, may suggest one principle. So far as the end of such competitions is good, the normal motives cannot be bad. The end of a fair competition is the discovery of the ablest men, with a view to placing them in the position where their talents may be turned to most account. It can only be achieved so far as each man does his best to train his own powers, and is prepared to test them fairly against the powers of others. To work for that end is, then, not only permissible, but a duty. The spirit in which the end is pursued may be bad, in so far as a man pursues it by unfair means; in so far as he tries to make sham performance pass off for genuine; or, again, in so far as he sets an undue value upon the reward, as apart from the qualities by which it is gained. But if he works simply with the desire of making the best of himself, and if the reward is simply such a position as may enable him to be most useful to society, the competition which results will be bracing and invigorating, and will appeal to no such motives as can be called, in the bad sense, selfish. He is discharging a function which is useful, it is true, to himself; but which is also intrinsically useful to the whole society. The same principle applies, again, to intellectual activity in general. All genuine thought is essentially useful to mankind. In the struggle to discover truth, even our antagonists are, necessarily, our co-operators. A philosopher, as a man of science, owes, at least, as much to those who differ from him, as to those who agree with him. The conflict of many minds, from many sides, is the essential condition of intellectual progress. Now, if a man plays his part manfully and honourably in such a struggle, he deserves our gratitude, even if he takes the wrong side. If he looks forward to the recognition by the best judges as one motive for his activity, I think that he is asking for a worthy reward. He deserves blame, only so far as his motives have a mixture of unworthy personal sentiment. Obviously, if he aims at cheap fame, at making a temporary sensation instead of a permanent impression, at flattering prejudices instead of spreading truth; or, if he shows greediness of notoriety, by trying to get unjust credit, as we sometimes see scientific people squabbling over claims to the first promulgation of some trifling discovery, he is showing paltriness of spirit. The men whom we revere are those who, like Faraday or Darwin, devoted themselves exclusively to the advancement of knowledge, and would have scorned a reputation won by anything but genuine work. The fact that there is a competition in such matters implies, no doubt, a temptation,-the temptation to set a higher value upon praise than upon praiseworthiness; but I think it not only possible that the competitors in such rivalries may keep to the honourable path, but probable that, as a matter of fact, they frequently,-I hope that I may say generally,-do so. If the fame at which a man aims be not that which "in broad rumour lies," but that which "lives and spreads aloft in those pure eyes and perfect witness of all-judging Jove," then I think that the desire for it is scarcely to be called a last infirmity-rather, it is an inseparable quality of noble minds. We wish to honour men who have been good soldiers in that warfare, and we can hardly wish them to be indifferent to our homage.

We may add, then, that a competition need not be demoralising when the competitors have lofty aims and use only honourable means. When, passing from purely intellectual aims, we consider the case, say, of the race for wealth, we may safely make an analogous remark. If a man's aim in becoming rich is of the vulgar kind; if he wishes to make an ostentatious display of wealth, and to spend his money upon demoralising amusement; or if, again, he tries to succeed by quackery instead of by the production of honest work, he is, of course, so far mischievous and immoral. But a man whose aims are public-spirited, nay, even if they be such as simply tend to improve the general comfort; who develops, for example, the resources of the country, and introduces new industries or more effective modes of manufacture, is, undoubtedly, in fact conferring a benefit upon his fellows, and may, so far, be doing his duty in the most effectual way open to him. If he succeeds by being really a more efficient man of business than his neighbours, he is only doing what, in the interests of all, it is desirable that he should do. He is discharging an essential social function; and what is to be desired is, that he should feel the responsibility involved, that he should regard his work as on one side the discharge of a social function, and not simply as a means of personal aggrandisement. It is not the fact that he is competing that is against him; but the fact, when it is a fact, that there is something discreditable about the means which he adopts, or the reward that he contemplates.

This, indeed, suggests another and a highly important question-the question, namely, whether, in our present social state, his reward may not be excessive, and won at too great a cost to his rivals. And, without going into other questions involved, I will try to say a little, in conclusion, upon this, which is certainly a pressing problem. Competition, I have suggested, is not immoral if it is a competition in doing honest work by honourable means, and if it is also a fair competition. But it must, of course, be added, that fairness includes more than the simple equality of chances. It supposes, also, that there should be some proportion between the rewards and the merits. If it is simply a question between two men, which shall be captain of a ship, and which shall be mate, then the best plan is to decide by their merits as sailors; and, if their merits be fairly tried, the loser need bear no grudge against the winner. But when we have such cases as sometimes occur, when, for example, the ship is cast away, and it becomes a question whether I shall eat you or you shall eat me, or, let us say, which of us is to have the last biscuit, we get one of those terrible cases of temptation in which the strongest social bonds sometimes give way under the strain. The competition, then, becomes, in the highest degree, demoralising, and the struggle for existence resolves itself into a mere unscrupulous scramble for life, at any sacrifice of others. That, it is sometimes said, is a parallel to our social state at present. If I gave an excessive prize to the first boy in a school and flogged the second, I should not be doing justice. If one man is rewarded for a moderate amount of forethought by becoming a millionaire, and his unsuccessful rivals punished by starvation or the workhouse, the lottery of life is not arranged on principles of justice. A man must be a very determined optimist if he denied the painful truth to be found in such statements. He must be blind to many evils if he does not perceive the danger of dulling his sympathies by indifference to the fate of the unsuccessful. The rich man in Clough's poem observes that, whether there be a God matters very little-

For I and mine, thank somebody,

Manage to get our victual.

But, even if we are not very rich, we must often, I think, doubt whether we are not wrapping ourselves in a spirit of selfish complacency when we are returning to a comfortable home and passing outcasts of the street. We must sometimes reflect that our comfort is not simply a reward for virtue or intelligence, even if it be not sometimes the prize of actual dishonesty. To shut our eyes to the mass of wretchedness around us is to harden our hearts, although to open our hands is too often to do more harm than good. It is no wonder that we should be tempted to declaim against competition, when the competition means that so many unfortunates are to be crowded off their narrow standing-ground into the gulf of pauperism.

This may suggest the moral which I have been endeavouring to bring out. Looking at society at large, we may surely say that it will be better in proportion as every man is strenuously endeavouring to play his part, and in which the parts are distributed to those best fitted to play them. We must admit, too, that for any period to which we can look forward, the great mass of mankind will find enough to occupy their energies in labouring primarily for their own support, and so bearing the burden of their own needs and the needs of their families. We may infer, too, that a society will be the better so far as it gives the most open careers to all talents, wherever displayed, and as it shows respect for the homely virtues of industry, integrity, and forethought, which are essential to the whole body as to its constituent members. And we may further say that the corresponding motives in the individual cannot be immoral. A desire of independence, the self-respect which makes a man shrink from accepting as a gift what he can win as a fair reward, the love of fairplay, which makes him use only honest means in the struggle, are qualities which can never lose their value, and which are not the less valuable because in the first instance they are most profitable to their possessors. Nothing which tends to weaken such motives can be good; but while they preserve their intensity, they necessarily imply the existence of competition in some form or other.

It is equally clear that competition by itself is not a sufficient panacea. Whenever we take an abstract quality, personify it by the help of capital letters, and lay it down as the one principle of a complex system, we generally blunder. Competition is as far as possible from being the solitary condition of a healthy society. It must be not only a competition for worthy ends by honourable means, but should be a competition so regulated that the reward may bear some proportion to the merit. Monopoly is an evil in so far as it means an exclusive possession of some advantages or privileges, especially when they are given by the accidents of birth or position. It is something if they are given to the best and the ablest; but the evil still remains if even the best and ablest are rewarded by a position which cramps the energies and lowers the necessity of others. Competition is only desirable in so far as it is a process by which the useful qualities are encouraged by an adequate, and not more than an adequate, stimulus; and in which, therefore, there is not involved the degradation and the misery on the one side, the excessive reward on the other, of the unsuccessful and the successful in the struggle. Competition, therefore, we might say, could be unequivocally beneficial only in an ideal society; in a state in which we might unreservedly devote ourselves to making the best of our abilities and accepting the consequent results, without the painful sense in the background that others were being sacrificed and debased; crushed because they had less luck in the struggle, and were, perhaps, only less deserving in some degree than ourselves. So long as we are still far enough from having realised any such state; so long as we feel, and cannot but feel, that the distribution of rewards is so much at the mercy of chance, and so often goes to qualities which, in an ideal state, would deserve rather reprobation than applause, we can only aim at better things. We can do what in us lies to level some inequalities, to work, so far as our opportunities enable us, in the causes which are mostly beneficial for the race, to spread enlightenment and good feeling, and to help the unfortunate. But it is also incumbent upon us to remember carefully, what is so often overlooked in the denunciations of competition, that the end for which we must hope, and the approach to which we must further, is one in which the equivocal virtue of charity shall be suppressed; that is, in which no man shall be dependent upon his neighbour in such a sense as to be able to neglect his own duties; in which there may be normally a reciprocity of good services, and the reciprocity not be (as has been said) all on one side. There is a very explicable tendency at present to ask for such one-sided reciprocity. It is natural enough, for reasons too obvious to be mentioned, that reformers should dwell exclusively upon the right of every one to support, and neglect to point out the correlative duty of every one to do his best to support himself. The popular arguments about "old-age pensions" may illustrate the general state of mind. It is disgraceful, people say, that so large a proportion of the aged poor should come to depend upon the rates. Undoubtedly it is disgraceful. Then upon whom does the disgrace fall? It sounds harsh to say that it falls upon the sufferers. We shrink from saying to a pauper, "It serves you right". That sounds brutal, and is only in part true. Still, we should not shrink from stating whatever is true, painful though it may be. It sounds better to lay all the blame upon the oppressor than to lay it upon the oppressed; and yet, as a rule, the cowardice or folly of the oppressed has generally been one cause of their misfortunes, and cannot be overlooked in a true estimate of the case. That drunkenness, improvidence, love of gambling, and so forth, do in fact lead to pauperism is undeniable; and that they are bad, and so far disgraceful, is a necessary consequence. In such cases, then, pauperism is a proof of bad qualities; and the fact, like all other facts, must be recognised. The stress of argument, therefore, is laid upon the hardships suffered by the honest and industrious poor. The logical consequence should be, that the deserving poor should become pensioners, and the undeserving paupers. This at once opens the amazingly difficult question of moral merit, and the power of poor-law officials to solve problems which would certainly puzzle the keenest psychologists. Suppose, for example, that a man, without being definitely vicious, has counted upon the promised pension, and therefore neglected any attempts to save. If you give him a pension, you virtually tell everybody that saving is a folly; if you don't, you inflict upon him the stigma which is deserved by the drunkard and the thief. So difficult is it to arrange for this proposed valuation of a man's moral qualities that it has been proposed to get rid of all stigma by making it the right and duty of every one to take a pension. That might conceivably alter the praise, but it would surely not alter the praiseworthiness. It must be wrong in me to take money from my neighbours when I don't want it; and, if wrong, it surely ought to be disgraceful. And this seems to indicate the real point. We may aim at altering the facts, at making them more conducive to good qualities; but we cannot alter or attempt to decide by laws the degree of praise or blame to be attached to individuals. It would be very desirable to bring about a state of things in which no honest and provident man need ever fall into want; and, in that state, pauperism would be rightly discreditable as an indication of bad qualities. But to say that nobody shall be ashamed of taking support would be to ruin the essential economic virtues, and to pauperise the nation; and to try to lay down precise rules as to the distribution of honour and discredit, seems, to me, to be a problem beyond the power of a legislature. I express no opinion upon the question itself, because I am quite incompetent to do so. I only refer to it as illustrating the difficulties which beset us when we try to remove the evils of the present system, and yet to preserve the stimulus to industry, which is implied in competition. The shortest plan is to shut one's eyes to the difficulty, and roundly deny its existence. I hope that our legislators may hit upon some more promising methods. The ordinary mode of cutting the knot too often suggests that the actually contemplated ideal is the land in which the chickens run about ready roasted, and the curse of labour is finally removed from mankind. The true ideal, surely, is the state in which labour shall be generally a blessing; in which we shall recognise the fact-disagreeable or otherwise-that the race can only be elevated by the universal diffusion of public spirit, and a general conviction that it is every man's first duty to cultivate his own capacities, to turn them to the best possible account, and to work strenuously and heartily in whatever position he has been placed. It is because I cannot help thinking that when we attack competition in general terms, we are, too often, blinding ourselves to those homely and often-repeated, and, as I believe, indisputable truths, that I have ventured to speak to-day, namely, on the side of competition-so far, at least, on the side of competition as to suggest that our true ideal should be, not a state, if such a state be conceivable, in which there is no competition, but a state in which competition should be so regulated that it should be really equivalent to a process of bringing about the best possible distribution of the whole social forces; and should be held to be, because it would really be, not a struggle of each man to seize upon a larger share of insufficient means, but the honest effort of each man to do the very utmost he can to make himself a thoroughly efficient member of society.

SOCIAL EQUALITY

The problem of which I propose to speak is the old dispute between Dives and Lazarus. Lazarus, presumably, was a better man than Dives. How could Dives justify himself for living in purple and fine linen, while Lazarus was lying at the gates, with the dogs licking his sores? The problem is one of all ages, and takes many forms. When the old Puritan saw a man going to the gallows, "There," he said, "but for the grace of God, goes John Bradford". When the rich man, entering his club, sees some wretched tatterdemalion, slouching on the pavement, there, he may say, goes Sir Gorgius Midas, but for-what? I am here and he there, he may say, because I was the son of a successful stock-jobber, and he the son of some deserted mother at the workhouse. That is the cause, but is it a reason? Suppose, as is likely enough, that Lazarus is as good a man as Midas, ought they not to change places, or to share their property equally? A question, certainly, to be asked, and, if possible, to be answered.

It is often answered, and is most simply answered, by saying that all men ought to be equal. Dives should be cut up and distributed in equal shares between Lazarus and his brethren. The dogma which embodies this claim is one which is easily refuted in some of the senses which it may bear, though in spite of such refutations it has become an essential part of the most genuine creed of mankind. The man of science says, with perfect truth, that so far from men being born equal, some are born with the capacity of becoming Shakespeares and Newtons, and others with scarcely the power of rising above Sally the chimpanzee. The answer would be conclusive, if anybody demanded that we should all be just six feet high, with brains weighing sixty ounces, neither more nor less. It is also true, and, I conceive, more relevant, that, as the man of science will again say, all improvement has come through little groups of men superior to their neighbours, through races or through classes, which, by elevating themselves on the shoulders of others, have gained leisure and means for superior cultivation. But equality may be demanded as facilitating this process, by removing the artificial advantages of wealth. It may be taken as a demand for a fair start, not as a demand that the prizes shall be distributed irrespectively of individual worth. And, whether the demand is rightly or wrongly expressed, we must, I think, admit that the real force with which we have to reckon is the demand for justice and for equality as somehow implied by justice. It is easy to browbeat a poor man who wants bread and cheese for himself and his family, by calling his demands materialistic, and advising him to turn his mind to the future state, where he will have the best of Dives. It is equally easy to ascribe the demands to mere envy and selfishness, or to those evil-minded agitators who, for their own wicked purposes, induce men to prefer a guinea to a pound of wages. But, after all, there is something in the demand for fair play and for the means of leading decent lives, which requires a better answer. It is easy, again, to say that all Socialists are Utopian. Make every man equal to-day, and the old inequalities will reappear to-morrow. Pitch such a one over London Bridge, it was said, with nothing on but his breeches, and he will turn up at Woolwich with his pockets full of gold. It is as idle to try for a dead level, when you work with such heterogeneous materials, as to persuade a homogeneous fluid to stand at anything but a dead level. But surely it may be urged that this is as much a reason for declining to believe that equal conditions of life will produce mere monotony, as for insisting that equality in any state is impossible. The present system includes a plan for keeping the scum at the surface. One of the few lessons which I have learnt from life, and not found already in copy-books, is the enormous difficulty which a man of the respectable classes finds in completely ruining himself, even by vice, extravagance, and folly; whereas, there are plenty of honest people who, in spite of economy and prudence, can scarcely keep outside of the workhouse. Admitting the appeal to justice, it is, again, often urged that justice is opposed to the demand for equality. Property is sacred, it is said, because a man has (or ought to have) a right to what he has made either by labour or by a course of fair dealings with other men. I am not about to discuss the ultimate ground on which the claim to private property is justified, and, as I think, satisfactorily established. A man has a right, we say, to all that he has fairly earned. Has he, then, a right to inherit what his father has earned? A man has had the advantage of all that a rich father can do for him in education, and so forth. Why should he also have the father's fortune, without earning it? Are the merits of making money so great that they are transmissible to posterity? Should a man who has been so good as to become rich, be blessed even to the third and fourth generation? Why, as a matter of pure justice, should not all fortunes be applied to public uses, on the death of the man who made them? Such a law, however impolitic, would not be incompatible with the moral principle to which an appeal is made. There are, of course, innumerable other ways in which laws may favour an equality of property, without breaking any of the fundamental principles. What, for example, is the just method of distributing taxation? A rich man can not only pay more money than a poor man, in proportion to his income, but he can, with equal ease, pay a greater proportion. To double the income of a labourer may be to raise him from starvation to comfort. To double the income of a millionaire may simply be to encumber him with wealth by which he is unable to increase his own pleasure. There is a limit beyond which it is exceedingly difficult to find ways of spending money on one's own enjoyment-though I have never been able to fix it precisely. On this ground, such plans as a graduated income-tax are, it would seem, compatible with the plea of justice; and, within certain limits, we do, in fact, approve of various taxes, on the ground, real or supposed, that they tend to shift burdens from the poor to the rich, and, so far, to equalise wealth. In fact, this appeal to justice is a tacit concession of the principle. If we justify property on the ground that it is fair that a man should keep what he has earned by his own labour, it seems to follow that it is unjust that he should have anything not earned by his labour. In other words, the answer admits the ordinary first principle from which Socialism starts, and which, in some Socialist theories, it definitely tries to embody.

All that I have tried to do, so far, is to show that the bare doctrine of equality, which is in some way connected with the demand for justice, is not, of necessity, either unjust or impracticable. It may be used to cover claims which are unjust, to sanction bare confiscation, to take away motives for industry, and, briefly, may be a demand of the drones to have an equal share of the honey. From the bare abstract principle of equality between men, we can, in my own opinion, deduce nothing; and, I do not think that the principle can itself be established. That is why it is made a first principle, or, in other words, one which is not to be discussed. The French revolutionists treated it in this way as à priori and self-evident. No school was in more deadly opposition to such à priori truths than the school of Bentham and the utilitarians. Yet, Bentham's famous doctrine, that in calculating happiness each man is to count for one, and nobody for more than one, seems to be simply the old principle in a new disguise. James Mill applied the doctrine to politics. J. S. Mill again applied it, with still more thoroughness, especially in his doctrine of representation and of the equality of the sexes. Accordingly, various moralists have urged that this was an inconsistency in utilitarian doctrine, implying that they, too, could make à priori first principles when they wanted them. It has become a sort of orthodox dogma with radicals, who do not always trouble themselves about a philosophical basis, and is applied with undoubting confidence to many practical political problems. "One man, one vote" is not simply the formulation of a demand, but seems to intimate a logical ground for the demand. If, in politics, one man is rightfully entitled to one vote, is it not also true that, in economics, one man should have a right to one income, or, that money, like political power, should be distributed into precisely equal shares? Yet, why are we to take for granted the equality of men in the sense required for such deductions? Since men are not equally qualified for political power, it would seem better primâ facie that each man should have the share of power and wealth which corresponds to his powers of using, or, perhaps, to his powers of enjoying. Why should we not say, "To each man according to his deserts"? One practical reason, of course, is the extreme difficulty of saying what are the deserts, and how they are to be ascertained. Undoubtedly, equality is the shortest and simplest way but, if we take it merely as the most convenient assumption, it loses its attractive appearance of abstract justice or à priori self-certainty. Do a common labourer and Mr. Gladstone deserve the same share of voting power? If not, how many votes should Mr. Gladstone possess to give him his just influence? To ask such questions is to show that answering is impossible, though political theorists have, now and then, tried to put together some ostensible pretext for an answer.

What, let us ask, is the true relation between justice and equality? A judge, to take the typical case, is perfectly just when he ascertains the facts by logical inferences from the evidence, and then applies the law in the spirit of a scientific reasoner. Given the facts, what is the rule under which they come? To answer that question, generally speaking, is his whole duty. In other words, he has to exclude all irrelevant considerations, such as his own private interests or affections. The parties are to be to him merely A and B, and he has to work out the result as an arithmetician works out a sum. Among the irrelevant considerations are frequently some moral aspects of the case. A judge, for example, decides a will to be valid or invalid without asking whether the testator acted justly or unjustly in a moral sense, but simply whether his action was legal or illegal. He cannot go behind the law, even from motives of benevolence or general maxims of justice, without being an unjust judge. Cases may arise, indeed, as I must say in passing, in which this is hardly true. A law may be so flagrantly unjust that a virtuous judge would refuse to administer it. One striking case was that of the fugitive slave law in the United States, where a man had to choose between acting legally and outraging humanity. So we consider a parent unjust who does not leave his fortune equally among his children. Unless there should be some special reason to the contrary, we shall hold him to be unfair for making distinctions out of mere preference of one child to another. Yet in the case of primogeniture our opinion would have to be modified. Supposing, for example, a state of society in which primogeniture was generally recognised as desirable for public interests, we could hardly call a man unjust for leaving his estates to his eldest son. If, in such a state, a man breaks the general rule, our judgment of his conduct would be determined perhaps by considering whether he was before or behind his age, whether he was acting from a keener perception of the evils of inequality or actuated by spite or regardless of the public interests which he believed to be concerned. A parent treats his children equally in his will in regard to money; but he does not, unless he is a fool, give the same training or the same opening to all his children, whether they are stupid or clever, industrious or idle. But what I wish to insist upon is, that justice implies essentially indifference to irrelevant considerations, and therefore, in many cases, equality in the treatment of the persons concerned. A judge has to decide without reference to bribes, and not be biassed by the position of an accused person. In that sense he treats the men equally, but of course he does not give equal treatment to the criminal and innocent, to the rightful and wrongful claimant.

The equality implied in justice is therefore to be understood as an exclusion of the irrelevant, and thus supposes an understanding as to what is irrelevant. It is not a mere abstract assertion of equality; but the assertion that, in a given concrete case, a certain rule is to be applied without considering anything outside of the rule. An ideally perfect rule would contain within itself a sufficient indication of what is to be relevant. All men of full age, sound mind, and so forth, are to be treated in such and such a way. Then all cases falling within the rule are to be decided on the same principles, and in that sense equally. But the problem remains, what considerations should be taken into account by the rule itself? Let us put the canon of equality in a different shape, namely, that there should always be a sufficient reason for any difference in the treatment of our fellows. This rule does not imply that I should act in all cases as though all men were equal in character or mind, but that my action should in all cases be justified by some appropriate consideration. It does not prove that every man should have a vote, but that if one man has a vote and another has not, there should be some adequate reason for the difference. It does not prove that every man should work eight hours a day and have a shilling an hour; but that differences of hours or of pay and, equally, uniformity of hours and pay, should have some sufficient justification. This is a deeper principle, which in some cases justifies and in others does not justify the rule of equality. The rule of equality follows from it under certain conditions, and has gained credit because, in point of fact, those conditions have often been satisfied.

The revolutionary demand for equality was, historically speaking, a protest against arbitrary inequality. It was a protest against the existence of privileges accompanied by no duties. When the rich man could only answer the question, "What have you done to justify your position?" by the famous phrase of Beaumarchais, "I took the trouble to be born," he was obviously in a false position. The demand for a society founded upon reason, in this sense that a sufficient reason should be given for all differences, was, it seems to me, perfectly right; and, moreover, was enough to condemn the then established system. But when this demand has been so constructed as to twist a logical rule, applicable to all scientific reasoning, into a dogmatic assertion that certain concrete beings were in fact equal, and to infer that they should have equal rights, it ceased to be logical at all, and has been a fruitful parent of many fallacies. Reasonable beings require a sufficient reason for all differences of conduct, for the difference between their treatment of a man and a monkey or a white man and a black, as well as for differences between treatment of rich and poor or wise men and fools; and there must, as the same principle implies, be also a sufficient reason for treating all members of a given class equally. We have to consider whether, for any given purpose, the differences between human beings and animals, Englishmen and negroes, men and women, are or are not of importance for our purpose. When the differences are irrelevant we neglect them or admit the claim to equality of treatment. But the question as to relevance is not to be taken for granted either way. It would be a very convenient but a very unjustifiable assumption in many cases, as it might save an astronomer trouble if he assumed that every star was equal to every other star.

The application of this is, I think, obvious. The â priori assumption of the equality of men is, in some sense, easily refuted. But the refutation does not entitle us to assume that arbitrary inequality, inequality for which no adequate ground can be assigned, is therefore justifiable. It merely shows that the problem is more complex than has been assumed at first sight. "All men ought to be equal." If you mean equal in natural capacity or character, it is enough to say that what is impossible cannot be. If you propose that the industrious and idle, the good and bad, the wise and foolish, should share equally in social advantages, the reply is equally obvious, that such a scheme, if possible, would be injurious to the qualities on which human welfare depends. If you say that men should be rewarded solely according to their intrinsic merits, we must ask, do you mean to abstract from the adventitious advantages of education, social surroundings, and so forth, or to take men as they actually are, whatever the circumstances to which their development is owing? To ask what a man would have been had he been in a different position from his youth, is to ask for an impossible solution, and one, moreover, of no practical bearing. I shall not employ a drunkard if I am in want of a butler, whether he has become a drunkard under overpowering temptation or become a drunkard from inherited dipsomania. But if, on the other hand, I take the man for what he is, without asking how he has come to be what he is, I leave the source at least of all the vast inequalities of which we complain. The difficulty, which I will not try to develop further, underlies, as I think, the really vital difference of method by which different schools attempt to answer the appeal for social justice.

The school of so-called individualists finds, in fact, that equality in their sense is incompatible with the varied differences due to the complete growth of the social structure. They look upon men simply as so many independent units of varying qualities, no doubt, but still capable of being considered for political and social purposes as equal. They ask virtually what justice would demand if we had before us a crowd of independent applicants for the good things of the world, and the simplest answer is to distribute the good things equally. If it is replied that the idle and the industrious should not be upon the same footing, they are ready to agree, perhaps, that men should be rewarded according to their services to society, however difficult it may be to arrange the proportions. But it soon appears that the various classes into which society is actually divided imply differences not due to the individual and his intrinsic merits, but to the varying surroundings in which he is placed. To do justice, then, it becomes necessary to get rid of these differences. The extreme case is that of the family. Every one probably owes more to his mother and to his early domestic environment than to any other of the circumstances which have influenced his development. If you and I started as perfectly equal babies, and you have become a saint and I a sinner, the divergence probably began when our mothers watched our cradles, and was made inevitable before we had left their knees. Consequently, the more thorough-going designers of Utopia have proposed to abolish this awkward difference. Men must be different at their birth; but we might conceivably arrange public nurseries which should place them all under approximately equal conditions. Then any differences would result from a man's intrinsic qualities, and he might be said to be rewarded simply according to his own merits.

The plan may be tempting, but has its disadvantages. There are injustices, if we call all inequality injustice, which we can only attribute to nature or to the unknown power which makes men and monkeys, Shakespeares and Stephens. And one result is that the character and conduct of human beings depend to a great extent upon circumstances, which are accidental in the sense that they are circumstances other than the original endowment of the individual. In this sense, maternal love, for example, is unjust. The mother loves her child because it is her own, not because it is better (though of course it is better) than other children. So, as Adam Smith, I think, observed, we are more moved by our neighbour's suffering from a corn on his great toe than by the starvation of millions in China. In other words, the affections, which are the great moving forces of society, are unjust in so far as they cause us to be infinitely more interested in our own little circle than in the remoter members of humanity known to us only by report. Without discussing the "justice" of this arrangement, we shall have, I think, to admit that it is inevitable. For I, at least, hold that the vague and vast organism of humanity depends for its cohesion upon the affinities and attractions, and not vice versâ. My interests are strongest where my power of action is greatest. The love of mothers for children is a force of essential value, and therefore to be cultivated rather than repressed, for no force known to us could replace it. And what is pre-eminently true in this case is, of course, true to a degree in others. Burke stated this with admirable force in his attack upon the revolutionists who expounded the opposite principle of abstract equality. "To be attached to the subdivision, to love the little platoon we belong to in society, is the first principle," he says, "the germ, as it were, of public affections. It is the first link in the series by which we proceed towards a love to our country and mankind." The assertion that they desired to invert this order, to destroy every social link in so far as it tended to produce inequalities, was the pith of his great indictment against the French "metaphysical" revolutionists. They had perverted the general logical precept of the sufficient reason for all inequalities by converting it into an assuming of the equality of concrete units. They fell into the fallacy of which I have spoken; and many radicals, utilitarians, and others have followed them. They assumed that all the varieties of human character, or all those due to the influence of the social environment, through whose structure and inherited instincts every full-grown man has been moulded, might be safely disregarded for the purpose of political and social construction. They have spoken, in brief, as if men were the equal and homogeneous atoms of physical inquiry and social problems capable of solution by a simple rearrangement of the atoms in different orders, instead of remembering that they are dealing with a complex organism, in which not only the whole order but every constituent atom is also a complex structure of indefinitely varying qualities. In the recognition of this truth lies, as I believe, the true secret of any satisfactory method of treatment.

Does this fact justify inequality in general? Or does not the principle of equality still remain as essentially implied in the Utopia which we all desire to construct? We have to take it for granted that to each man the first and primary moving instinct is and must be the love of the little "platoon" of which he is a member; that the problem is, not to destroy all these minor attractions, to obliterate the structure and replace society by a vast multitude of independent atoms, each supposed to aim directly at the good of the whole, but so to harmonise and develop or restrain the smaller interests of families, of groups and associations, that they may spontaneously co-operate towards the general welfare. It is a long and difficult task to which we have to apply ourselves; a task not to be effected by the demonstration or application of a single abstract dogma, but to be worked out gradually by the co-operation of many classes and of many generations. If it is fairly solved in the course of a thousand years or so, I for one shall be very fairly satisfied. But distant as the realisation may be, we may or rather ought to consider seriously the end to which we should be working. The conception implies a distinction of primary importance towards any clear treatment of the problem. We have, that is, two different, though not altogether distinct, provinces of what I may, perhaps, call organic and functional morality. We may take the existing order for granted, and ask what is then our duty; or we may ask how far the structure itself requires modification, and, if so, what kind of modification. A man who assumes the existence of the present structure may act justly or unjustly within the limits so prescribed. He must generally be guided in a number of cases by some principle of equality. The judge should endeavour to give the same law to rich and poor; the parent should not make arbitrary distinctions between his children; the statesman should try to distribute his burdens without favouring one particular class, and so forth. A man who, in such a sense, acts justly may be described as up to the level of his age and its accepted established moral ideas, and is, therefore, entitled at least to the negative praise of not being corrupt or dishonest. He fulfils accurately the functions imposed upon him, and is not governed by what Bentham called the sinister interests which would prevent them from being effectually discharged for the welfare of the community. But the problem which we have to consider is the deeper and more difficult one of organic justice; and our question is what justice means in this case, or what are the irrelevant considerations to be excluded from our motives of conduct.

Between these two classes of justice there are distinctions which it is necessary to state briefly. Justice, as we generally use the word, implies that the unjust man deserves to be hanged, or, at least, is responsible for his actions. What "responsibility" precisely implies is, of course, a debatable question. I only need assume that, in any case, it implies that somebody is guilty of wrong-doing, for which he should receive an appropriate penalty. But in organic questions it is not the individual, but the race which is responsible; and we require a reform, not a penalty. An impatient temper leads us to generalise too hastily from the case of the individual to that of the country. We bestow the blame for all the wrongs of an oppressed nation, for example, upon the nation which oppresses. But in simple point of fact, the oppressed nation generally deserves (if the word can be fairly used) to share the blame. The trodden worm would not have been trodden upon if it had been a bit of a viper. Whatever the duty of turning the second cheek, it is clearly not a national duty. If we admire a Tell or Robert Bruce for resisting oppressors, we implicitly condemn those who submitted to oppressors. If a nation is divided or wanting in courage, public spirit, and independence, it will be trampled down; and though we may most rightfully blame the tramplers, it is idle to exonerate the trampled. It is easy, in the same way, to make the rich solely responsible for all the misery of the poor. The man who has got the booty is naturally regarded as the robber. But, speaking scientifically, that is, with the desire to state the plain facts, we must admit that if the poor are those who have gone to the wall in the struggle for wealth; then, whatever unjust weapons have been used in that struggle, the improvidence and vice and idleness have certainly been among the main causes of defeat. Here, as before, the question is not, who is to be punished? We can only settle that when dealing with individual cases. It is the question, what is the cause of certain evils? and here we must resist the temptation of supposing that the class which in some sense appears to profit by them, or, at least, to be exempt from them, has, therefore, any more to do with bringing them about than the class which suffers from them.

The reflection may put us in mind of what seems to be a general law. The ultimate cause of the adoption of institutions and rules of conduct is often the fact of their utility to the race; but it is only at a later period that their utility becomes the conscious or avowed reason for maintaining them. The political fabric has been clearly built up, in great part, by purely selfish ambition. Nations have been formed by energetic rulers, who had no eye for anything beyond the gratification of their own ambition, although they were clear-headed enough to see that their own ambition could best secure its objects by taking the side of the stronger social forces, and by giving substantial benefit to others. The same holds good pre-eminently of industrial relations. We all know how Adam Smith, sharing the philosophical optimism of his time, showed how the pursuit of his own welfare by each man tended, by a kind of pre-ordained harmony, to contribute to the welfare of all. Since his time we have ceased to be so optimistic, and have recognised the fact that the building up of modern industrial systems has involved much injury to large classes. And yet we may, I think, in great measure adopt his view. The fact that each man was rogue enough to think first of himself and of his own wife and family is not a proof or a presumption that he did not flourish because, in point of fact, he was contributing (quite unintentionally perhaps) to the comforts of mankind in general. What we have to reflect is that, while the bare existence of certain institutions gives a strong presumption of their utility, there is also a probability that when the utility becomes a conscious aim or a consciously adopted criterion of their advantage, they will require a corresponding modification intended to secure the advantages at a minimum cost of evil.

Premising these remarks as to the meaning of organic justice, we can now come to the question of equality. Justice in its ordinary sense may be regarded from one point of view as the first condition of the efficiency of the social organ. In saying that a judge is just, we imply that he is so far efficiently discharging his part in society-the due application of the law-without reference to irrelevant considerations. He is a machine which rightly parts the sheep and goats-taking the legal definition of goats and sheep-instead of putting some goats into the sheepfold, and vice versâ. That is, he secures the accurate application of the purely legal rule. Organic justice involves an application of the same principle because it equally depends upon the exclusion of irrelevant considerations. It implies such a distribution of functions and of maintenance as may secure the greatest possible efficiency of society towards some end in itself good. Society of course may be organised with great efficiency for bad or doubtful ends. A purely military organisation, however admirable for its purpose, may imply a sacrifice of the highest welfare of the nation. Assuming, however, the goodness of the end, the greatest efficiency is of course desirable. We may, for our purposes, assume that the efficiency of a nation regarded as a society for the production of wealth is a desirable end. There are, of course, many other purposes which must not be sacrificed to the production of wealth. But power of producing wealth, meaning roughly whatever contributes to the physical support and comfort of the nation, is undoubtedly a necessary condition of all other happiness. If we all starve we can have neither art nor science nor morality. What I mean, therefore, is that a nation is so far better as it is able to raise all necessary supplies with the least expenditure of labour, leaving aside the question how far the superfluous forces should be devoted to raising comparative luxuries or to some purely religious or moral or intellectual purposes. The perfect industrial organisation is, I shall assume, compatible with or rather a condition of a perfect organisation of other kinds. In the most general terms we have to consider what are the principles of social organisation, which of course implies a certain balance between the various organs and a thorough nutrition of all, while yet we may for a moment confine our attention to the purely industrial or economic part of the question. How, if at all, does the principle of equality or of social justice enter the problem?

We may assume, in the first place, from this point of view, that one most obvious condition is the absence of all purely useless structures, whether of the kind which we call "survivals" or such as may be called parasitic growths. The organ which has ceased to discharge corresponding functions is simply a drag upon the vital forces. When a class, such as the old French aristocracy, ceases to perform duties while retaining privileges, it will be removed,-too probably, as in that case, it will be removed by violent and mischievous methods,-if the society is to grow in vigour. The individuals, as I have said, may or may not deserve punishment, for they are not personally responsible for the general order of things; but they are not unlikely to incur severe penalties, and what we should really hope is that they may be in some way absorbed by judicious medical treatment, instead of extirpated by the knife. At the other end of the scale, we have the parasitic class of the beggars or thieves. They, too, are not personally responsible for the conditions into which they are born. But they are not only to be pitied individually, but to be regarded, in the mass, as involving social disease and danger. More words upon that topic are quite superfluous, but I may just recall the truth that the two evils are directly connected. We hear it often said, and often denied, that the rich are growing richer and the poor poorer. So far, however, as it is true, it is one version of the very obvious fact that where there are many careless rich people, there will be the best chance for the beggars. The thoughtless expenditure of the rich without due responsibilities, provides the steady stream of so-called charity,-the charity which, as Shakespeare (or somebody else) observes, is twice cursed, which curses him that gives and him that receives; which is to the rich man as a mere drug to still his conscience and offer a spurious receipt in full for his neglect of social duties, and to the poor man an encouragement to live without self-respect, without providence, a mere hanger-on and dead-weight upon society, and a standing injury and source of temptation to his honest neighbours.

Briefly, a wholesome social condition implies that every social organ discharges a useful function; it renders some service to the community which is equivalent to the support which it derives; brain and stomach each get their due share of supply; and there is a thorough reciprocity between all the different members of the body. But what kind of equality should be desired in order to secure this desirable organic balance? We have to do, I may remark, with the case of a homogeneous race. By this I mean not only that there is no reason to suppose that there is any difference between the innate qualities of rich and poor, but that there is the strongest reason for believing in an equality; that is to say, more definitely, that if you took a thousand poor babies and a thousand rich babies, and subjected them to the same conditions, they would show great individual differences, but no difference traceable to the mere difference of class origin. I therefore may leave aside such problems as might arise in the Southern States of America, or even in British India, where two different races are in presence; or, again, the case of the sexes, where we cannot assume as self-evident, that the organic differences are irrelevant to political or social ends. So far as we are concerned, we may take it for granted that the differences which emerge are not due to any causes antecedent to and overriding the differences due to different social positions. If we can say justly (as has been said) that a poor man is generally more charitable in proportion to his means, or, again, that he is, as a rule, a greater liar or a greater drunkard than the rich man, the difference is not due to a difference of breed, but to the education (in the widest sense) which each has received. So long as that difference remains, we must take account of it for purposes of obtaining the maximum efficiency. We must not make the poor man a professor of mathematics, or even manager of a railway, because he has talents which, if trained, would have qualified him for the post; but we may and must assume that an equal training would do as much for the poor man as for the rich; and the question is, how far it is desirable or possible to secure such equality.

Now, from the point of view of securing a maximum efficiency, it seems to be a clearly desirable end that the only qualities which should indisputably help to determine a man's position in life, should also be those which determine his fitness for working in it efficiently. In Utopia, it should be the rule that each man shall do what he can do best. If one man is a gamekeeper and another a prime minister, it should be because one has the gifts of a gamekeeper and the other the gifts of a prime minister: whereas, in the actual state, as we all know, the gamekeeper often becomes the prime minister, while the potential prime minister is limited to looking after poachers. But I also urge that we must take into account the actual and not the potential qualities at any given moment. The inequality may be obviated by raising the grade of culture in all classes; but we must not assume that there is an actual equality where, in fact, there is the widest possible difference. In short, I assert that it is our duty to try to make men equal; though I deny that we are clearly justified in assuming an equality. By making them equal, I do not, of course, mean that we should try to make them all alike. I recognise, with Mill and every sensible writer on the subject, that such a consummation represents rather a danger than an advantage. I wish to see individuality strengthened, not crushed, to encourage men to develop the widest possible diversity of tastes, talents, and pursuits, and to attain unity of opinion, not by a calm assumption that this or that creed is true, but by encouraging the sharpest and freest collision of opinions. The equality of which I speak is that which would result, if the distinction into organs were not of such a nature as to make one class more favourable than another to the full development of whatever character and talents a man may possess. In other words, the distribution into classes would correspond purely and simply to the telling off of each man to the duties which he is best fitted to discharge. The position into which he is born, the class surroundings which determine his development, must not carry with them any disqualification for his acquiring the necessary aptitude for any other position. It was, I think, Fourier who argued that a man ought to be paid more highly for being a chimney-sweep than for being a prime minister, because the duties of a sweep are the more disagreeable,-a position which some prime ministers may, perhaps, see reason to doubt. My suggestion is, that in Utopia every human being would be so placed as to be capable of preparing himself for any other position, and should then go to the work for which he is best fitted. The equality as thus defined would, I submit, leave no room for a sense of injustice, because the qualities which determine a man's position would be the qualities for which he deserves the position, desert in this sense being measurable by fitness. Discontent with class distinctions must arise so long as a man feels that his position in a class limits and cramps his capacities below the level of happier fortunes. Discontent is not altogether a bad thing, for it is often an alias for hope; remove all discontent and you remove all guarantee for improvement. But discontent is of the malignant variety when it is allied with a sense of injustice; that is, of restrictions imposed upon one class for no assignable reason. The only sufficient reason for classes is the efficient discharge of social functions. The differences between the positions of men in social strata, supply some of the most effective motives for the struggle of life; and the effort of men to rise into the wealthy or the powerful class is not likely to cease so long as men are men; but they take an unworthy form so long as the ambition is simply to attain privileges unconnected with or disproportioned to the duties involved, and which therefore generate hatred to the social structure. If a class could be simply an organ for the discharge of certain functions, and each man in the whole body politic able to fit himself for that class, the injustice, and therefore the malignant variety of discontent, would disappear. Of course, I am speaking only of justice. I do not attempt to define the proper ends of society, or regard justice in itself as a sufficient guarantee for all desirable results. Such justice may exist even in a savage tribe or a low social type. There may be a just distribution of food among a shipwrecked crew, but the attainment of such justice would not satisfy all their wants. The abolition of misery, the elevation of a degraded class to a higher stage is a good thing in itself, unless it can be shown to involve some counterbalancing evil. I only argue that the ideal society would have this, among other attributes, and, therefore, that to secure such equality is a legitimate object of aspiration.

I am speaking of "Utopia". The time is indefinitely distant when a man will choose to be a sweep or a prime minister according to his aptitudes, and be equally able to learn his trade whether he is the son of a prime minister or a sweep. I only try to indicate the goal to which our efforts should be directed. But the goal thus defined implies methods different from that of some advocates of equality. They propose at once to assume the non-existence of a disagreeable difficulty, and to take men as equal in a sense in which they are not, in fact, equal. To me the problem appears to be, not the instant introduction of a new system, but a necessarily long and very gradual process of education directed towards the distant goal of making men equal in the desirable sense; and that problem, I add, is in the main a moral problem. It is idle to make institutions without making the qualities by which they must be worked. I do not say-far from it-that we are not to propose what may roughly be called external changes: new regulations and new forms of association, and so forth. On the contrary, I believe, as I have intimated, that this method corresponds to the normal order of development. The new institution protects and stimulates the germs of the moral instincts by which it must be worked. But I also hold that no mere rearrangement does any permanent good unless it calls forth a corresponding moral change, and, moreover, that the moral change, however slow and imperceptible, does incomparably more than any external change.

If we assume our present institutions to be permanent, a slight improvement in moral qualities, a growth of sobriety, of chastity, of prudence and intellectual culture, would make an almost indefinite improvement in the condition of the masses. If, for example, Englishmen ceased to drink, every English home might be made reasonably comfortable. The two kinds of change imply each other; but it is the most characteristic error of the designers of Utopias to suppose a mere change of regulations without sufficiently attending to the moral implication. To attain equality, as I have tried to define the word, would imply vast moral changes, and therefore a long and difficult elaboration. We have not simply to make men happy, as they now count happiness, but to alter their views of happiness. The good old copy-books tell us that happiness is as common in poor men's huts as in rich men's palaces. We are apt to reply that the statement is a mockery and a lie. But it points to the consummation which in some simple social states has been partly realised, and which in some distant future may come to be an expression of facts. It is conceivable surely that rich men may some day find that there are modes of occupation which are more interesting as well as more useful than accumulation of luxuries or the keeping of horses for the turf; that, in place of propitiating fate by supporting the institution of beggary, there is an indefinite field for public-spirited energy in the way not of throwing crumbs to Lazarus, but of promoting national culture of mind, of spirit, and of body; that benevolence does not mean simple self-sacrifice, except to the selfish, but the pursuit of a noble and most interesting career; that men's duty to their children is not to enable them to lead idle lives, but to fit them for playing a manly part in the great game of life; and that their relation to those whom they employ is not that of persons exploiting the energies of inferior animals, but of leaders of industry with a common interest in the prosperity of their occupation. People, no doubt, will hardly pursue business from motives of pure benevolence to others, and I do not think it desirable that they should. But the recognition that the pursuit of an honourable business is useful to others may, nevertheless, guide their energies, make the mere scramble for wealth disreputable, and induce them to labour for solid and permanent advantages. Such moral changes are, I conceive, necessary conditions of the equality of which I have spoken; they must be brought about to some extent if the industrial organism is to free itself from the injustice necessarily implied in a mere blind struggle for personal comfort.

Moreover, however distant the final consummation may be, there are, I think, many indications of an approximation. Nothing is more characteristic of modern society than the enormous development of the power of association for particular purposes. In former days a society had to form an independent organ, a corporation, a college, and so forth, to discharge any particular function, and the resulting organ was so distinct as to absorb the whole life of its members. The work of the fellow was absorbed in the corporate life of his corporation, and he had no distinct personal interests. Now we are all members of societies by the dozen, and society is constantly acquiring the art of forming associations for any purpose, temporary or permanent, which imply no deep structural division, and unite people of all classes and positions. As the profounder lines are obliterated, the tendency to form separate castes, defended by personal privileges, and holding themselves apart from other classes, rapidly diminishes; and the corresponding prejudices are in process of diminution. But I can only hint at this principle.

A correlative moral change in the poor is, of course, equally essential. America is described by Mr. Lowell in the noblest panegyric ever made upon his own country, as "She that lifts up the manhood of the poor". She has taken some rather queer methods of securing that object lately; yet, however imperfect the result, every American traveller will, I believe, sympathise with what Mr. Bryce has recently said in his great book. America is still the land of hope-the land where the poor man's horizon is not bounded by a vista of inevitable dependence on charity; where-in spite of some superficially grotesque results-every man can speak to every other without the oppressive sense of condescension; where a civil word from a poor man is not always a covert request for a gratuity and a tacit confession of dependence. "Alas," says Wordsworth, in one of his pregnant phrases, "the gratitude of men has oftener left me mourning" than their cold-heartedness; because, I presume, it is a painful proof of the rarity of kindness. When one man can only receive a gift and another can only bestow it as a payment on account of a long accumulation of the arrears of class injustice, the relations hardly admit of genuine gratitude on either side. What grates most painfully upon me, and, I suppose, upon most of us, is the "servility" of man; the acceptance of a beggar's code of morals as natural and proper for any one in a shabby coat. The more prominent evil just now, according to conservatives and pessimists, is the correlative one of the beggar on horseback; of the man who has found out that he can squeeze more out of his masters, and uses his power even without considering whether it is wise to drain your milch cow too exhaustively.

A hope of better things is encouraged by schemes for arbitration and conciliation between employers and employed. But we require a moral change if arbitration is to imply something more than a truce between natural enemies, and conciliation to be something different from that employed by Hood's butcher when, after hauling a sheep by main force into the slaughter-house, he exclaimed, "There, I've conciliated him!" The only principle on which arbitration can proceed is that the profits should be divided in such a way as to be a sufficient inducement to all persons concerned to give their money or their labour, mental or physical, to promote the prosperity of the business at large. But the reconciliation can only be complete when the capitalist is capable of employing his riches with enough public spirit and generosity to disarm mere envy by his obvious utility, and the poor man justifies his increased wages by his desire to secure permanent benefits and a better standard of life. In Utopia, the question will still be, what plan shall be a sufficient inducement to the men who co-operate as employers or labourers, but the inducement will appeal to better motives, and the positions be so far equalised that each will be most tolerable to the man best fitted for it.

Here a vast series of problems opens about which I can only suggest the briefest hint. The principle I now urge is the old one, namely, that the usual mark of a quack remedy is the neglect of the moral aspect of a question. We want a state of opinion in which the poor are not objects to be slobbered over, but men to help in a manly struggle for moral as well as material elevation. A great deal is said, for example, about the evils of competition. It is remarkable indeed that few proposals for improvement even, so far as I can discover, tend to get rid of competition. Co-operation, as tradesmen will tell us, is not an abolition of competition, but a competition of groups instead of units. "Profit-sharing" is simply a plan by which workmen may take a direct share in the competition carried on by their masters. I do not mention this as any objection to such schemes, for I do not think that competition is an evil. I do not doubt the vast utility of schemes which tend to increase the intelligence and prudence of workmen, and give them an insight into the conditions of successful business. Competition is no doubt bad so far as it means cheating or gambling. But competition is, it seems to me, inevitable so long as we are forced to apply the experimental method in practical life, and I fail to see what other method is available. Competition means that thousands of people all over the world are trying to find out how they can supply more economically and efficiently the wants of other people, and that is a state of things to which I do not altogether object. Equality in my sense implies that every one should be allowed to compete for every place that he can fill. The cry is merely, as it seems to me, an evasion of the fundamental difficulty. That difficulty is not that people compete, but that there are too many competitors; not that a man's seat at the table has to be decided by fair trial of his abilities, but that there is not room enough to seat everybody. Malthus brought to the front the great stumbling-block in the way of Utopian optimism. His theory was stated too absolutely, and his view of the remedy was undoubtedly crude. But he hit the real difficulty; and every sensible observer of social evils admits that the great obstacle to social improvement is that social residuum, the parasitic class, which multiplies so as to keep down the standard of living, and turns to bad purposes the increased power of man over nature. We have abolished pestilence and famine in their grimmest shape; if we have not abolished war, it no longer involves usurpation or slavery or the permanent desolation of the conquered; but one result is just this, that great masses can be regularly kept alive at the lowest stage of existence without being periodically swept away by a "black death" or a horde of brutal invaders. If we choose to turn our advantages to account in this way, no nostrums will put an end to poverty; and the evil can only be met-as I venture to assume-by an elevation of the moral level, involving all that is implied in spreading civilisation downward.

The difficulty shows itself in discussions of the proper sphere of government. Upon that vast and most puzzling topic I will only permit myself one remark. In former times the great aim of reformers was the limitation of the powers of government. They came to regard it as a kind of bogy or extra-natural force, which acted to oppress the poor in order to maintain certain personal privileges. Some, like Godwin of the "Political Justice," held that the millennium implied the abolition of government and the institution of anarchy. The early utilitarians held that government might be reformed by placing power in the hands of the subjects, who would use it only for their own interests, but still retained the prejudices engendered in their long struggle against authority, and held that its functions should still be gradually restricted on pain of developing a worse tyranny than the old. The government has been handed over to the people as they desired, but with the natural result that the new authorities not only use it to support their interests, but retain the conviction of its extra-natural, or perhaps supernatural, efficacy. It is regarded as an omnipotent body which can not only say (as it can) that whatever it pleases shall be legal, but that whatever is made a law in the juridical sense shall at once become a law of nature. Even their individualist opponents, who profess to follow Mr. Herbert Spencer, seem often to regard the power of government, not as one result of evolution, but as something external which can constrain and limit evolution. It corresponds to a kind of outside pressure which interferes arbitrarily with the so-called natural course of development, and should therefore be abolished. To me, on the contrary, it seems that government is simply one of the social organs, with powers strictly limited by its relation to others and by the nature of the sentiment upon which it rests. There are obvious reasons, in the centralisation of vast industrial interests, the "integration," as Mr. Spencer calls it, which is the correlative of differentiation, in the growing solidarity of different classes and countries, in the consequent growth of natural monopolies, which give a solid reason for believing that the functions of the central government may require expansion. To decide by any à priori principle what should be the limits of this expansion is, to my mind, hopeless. The problem is one to be worked out by experiment,-that is, by many generations and by repeated blundering. A fool, said Erasmus Darwin, is a man who never makes an experiment; an experiment is a new mode of action which fails in its object ninety-nine times out of a hundred; therefore, wise men make more blunders, though they also make more discoveries than fools. Now, experiments in government and social organisation are as necessary to improvement as any other kind of experiment, and probably still more liable to failure. One thing, however, is again obvious. The simple remedy of throwing everything upon government, of allowing it to settle the rate of wages, the hours of labour, the prices of commodities, and so forth, requires for success a moral and intellectual change which it is impossible to over-estimate. I will not repeat the familiar arguments which, to my mind, justify this statement. It is enough to say that there is no ground in the bare proposal for putting all manner of industrial regulations into the hands of government, for supposing that it would not drag down every one into pauperism instead of raising everybody to comfort. I often read essays of which the weakness seems to be that while they purpose to establish equality, they give no real reason for holding that it would not be an equality of beggary. If every one is to be supported, idle or not, the natural conclusion is universal pauperism. If people are to be forced to work by government, or their numbers to be somehow restricted by government, you throw a stress upon the powers of government which, I will not say, it is impossible that it should bear, but which, to speak in the most moderate terms, implies a complete reconstruction of the intelligence, morality, and conceptions of happiness of human beings. Your government would have to be omniscient and purely benevolent as well as omnipotent, and I confess that I cannot see in the experience of those countries where the people have the most direct influence upon the government, any promise that this state of things will be realised just yet.

Thus, I return to my conclusion,-to my platitude, if you will. Professor Fawcett used to say that he could lay down no rules for the sphere of government influence, except this rule, that no interference would do good unless it helped people to help themselves. I think that the doctrine was characteristic of his good sense, and I fully subscribe to it. I heartily agree that equality in the sense I have given, is a most desirable ideal; I agree that we should do all that in us lies to promote it; I only say that our aims should be always in consistence with the principle that such equality is only possible and desirable in so far as the lowest classes are lifted to a higher standard, morally as well as physically. Of course, that implies approval of every variety of new institutions and laws, of co-operation, of profit sharing, of boards of conciliation, of educational and other bodies for carrying light into darkness and elevating popular standards of life: but always with the express condition that no such institution is really useful except as it tends to foster a genuine spirit of independence, and to supply the moral improvement without which no outward change is worth a button. This is a truism, you may say. Yet, when I read the proposals to get rid of poverty by summarily ordering people to be equal, or to extirpate pauperism by spending a million upon certain institutions for out-door relief, I cannot help thinking that it is a truism which requires to be enforced. The old Political Economy, you say, is obsolete; meaning, perhaps, that you do not mean to be bothered with its assertions; but the old Economists had their merits. They were among the first who realised the vast importance of deeper social questions; they were the first who tried to treat them scientifically; they were not (I hope) the last who dared to speak unpleasant truths, simply because they believed them and believed in their importance. Perhaps, indeed, they rather enjoyed the practice a little too much, and indulged in it a little too ostentatiously. Yet, I am sure that, on the whole, it was a very useful practice, and one which is now scarcely as common as it should be. People are more anxious to pick holes in their statement of economic laws than to insist upon the essential fact that, after all, there are laws, not "laws" made by Parliament, but laws of nature, which do, and will, determine the production and distribution of wealth, and the recognition of which is as important to human welfare as the recognition of physiological laws to the bodily health. Holding this faith, the old Economists were never tired of asserting what is the fundamental truth of so-called "individualism," that, after all we may say about the social development, the essential condition of all social improvement is not that we should have this or that system of regulations, but that the individual should be manly, self-respecting, doing his duty as well as getting his pay, and deeply convinced that nothing will do any permanent good which does not imply the elevation of the individual in his standards of honesty, independence, and good conduct. We can only say to Lazarus: "You are probably past praying for, and all we can do is to save you from starving, by any means which do not encourage other people to fall into your weaknesses; but we recognise the right of your class for any and every possible help that can be given towards making men of them, and putting them on their legs by teaching them to stand upright".

ETHICS AND THE STRUGGLE FOR EXISTENCE

In his deeply-interesting Romanes lecture, Professor Huxley has stated the opinion that the ethical progress of society depends upon our combating the "cosmic process" which we call the struggle for existence. Since, as he adds, we inherit the "cosmic nature" which is the outcome of millions of years of severe training, it follows that the "ethical nature" may count upon having to reckon with a tenacious and powerful enemy as long as the world lasts. This is not a cheerful prospect. It is, as he admits, an audacious proposal to pit the microcosm against the macrocosm. We cannot help fearing that the microcosm may get the worst of it. Professor Huxley has not fully expanded his meaning, and says much to which I could cordially subscribe. But I think that the facts upon which he relies admit or require an interpretation which avoids the awkward conclusion.

Pain and suffering, as Professor Huxley tells us, are always with us, and even increase in quantity and intensity as evolution advances. The fact had been recognised in remote ages long before theories of evolution had taken their modern form. Pessimism, from the time of the ancient Hindoo philosophers to the time of their disciple, Schopenhauer, has been in no want of evidence to support its melancholy conclusions. It would be idle to waste rhetoric in the attempt to recapitulate so familiar a position. Though I am not a pessimist, I cannot doubt that there is more plausibility in the doctrine than I could wish. Moreover, it may be granted that any attempt to explain or to justify the existence of evil is undeniably futile. It is not so much that the problem cannot be answered, as that it cannot even be asked in any intelligible sense. To "explain" a fact is to assign its causes-that is, to give the preceding set of facts out of which it arose. However far we might go backwards, we should get no nearer to perceiving any reason for the original fact. If we explain the fall of man by Adam's eating the apple, we are quite unable to say why the apple should have been created. If we could discover a general theory of pain, showing, say, that it implied certain physiological conditions, we shall be no nearer to knowing why those physiological conditions should have been what they are. The existence of pain, in short, is one of the primary data of our problem, not one of the accidents, for which we can hope in any intelligible sense to account. To give any "justification" is equally impossible. The book of Job really suggests an impossible, one may almost say a meaningless, problem. We can give an intelligible meaning to a demand for justice when we can suppose that a man has certain antecedent rights, which another man may respect or neglect. But this has no meaning as between the abstraction "nature" and the concrete facts which are themselves nature. It is unjust to meet equal claims differently. But it is not "unjust" in any intelligible sense that one being should be a monkey and another a man, any more than that part of me should be a hand and another head. The question would only arise if we supposed that the man and the monkey had existed before they were created, and had then possessed claims to equal treatment. The most logical theologians, indeed, admit that as between creature and creator there can be properly no question of justice. The pot and the potter cannot complain of each other. If the writer of Job had been able to show that the virtuous were rewarded and the vicious punished, he would only have transferred the problem to another issue. The judge might be justified, but the creator would be condemned. How can it be just to place a being where he is certain to sin, and then to damn him for sinning? That is the problem to which no answer can be given; and which already implies a confusion of ideas. We apply the conception of justice in a sphere where it is not applicable, and naturally fail to get any intelligible answer.

It is impossible to combine the conceptions of God as the creator and God as the judge; and the logical straits into which the attempt leads are represented by the endless free-will controversy. I will not now enter that field of controversy: and I will only indicate what seems to me to be the position which we must accept in any scientific discussion of our problem. Hume, as I think, laid down the true principle when he said that there could be no à priori proof of a matter of fact. An à priori truth is a truth which cannot be denied without self-contradiction, but there can never be a logical consideration in supposing the non-existence of any fact whatever. The ordinary appeal to the truths of pure mathematics is, therefore, beside the question. All such truths are statements of the precise equivalence of two propositions. To say that there are four things is also to say that there are two pairs of things: to say that there is a plane triangle is also to say that there is a plane trilateral. One statement involves the other, because the difference is not in the thing described, but in our mode of contemplating it. We, therefore, cannot make one assertion and deny the other without implicit contradiction. From such results, again, is evolved (in the logical sense of evolution) the whole vast system of mathematical truths. The complexity of that system gives the erroneous idea that we can, somehow, attain a knowledge of facts, independently of experience. We fail to observe that even the most complex mathematical formula is simply a statement of an exact equivalence of two assertions; and that, till we know by experience the truth of one statement, we can never infer the truth, in fact, of the other. However elaborate may be the evolutions of mathematical truth, they can never get beyond the germs out of which they are evolved. They are valid precisely because the most complex statement is always the exact equivalent of the simpler, out of which it is constructed. They remain to the end truths of number or truths of geometry. They cannot, by themselves, tell us that things exist which can be counted or which can be measured. The whole claim, however elaborate, still requires its point of suspension. We may put their claims to absolute or necessary truth as high as we please; but they cannot give us by themselves a single fact. I can show, for example, that a circle has an infinite number of properties, all of which are virtually implied in the very existence of a circle. But that the circle or that space itself exists, is not a necessary truth, but a datum of experience. It is quite true that such truths are not, in one sense, empirical; they can be discovered without any change of experience; for, by their very nature, they refer to the constant element of experience, and are true on the supposition of the absolute changelessness of the objects contemplated. But it is a fallacy to suppose that, because independent of particular experiences, they are, therefore, independent of experience in general.

Now, if we agree, as Huxley would have agreed, that Hume's doctrine is true, if we cannot know a single fact except from experience, we are limited in moral questions, as in all others, to elaborating and analysing our experience, and can never properly transcend it. A scientific treatment of an ethical question, at any rate, must take for granted all the facts of human nature. It can show what morality actually is; what are, in fact, the motives which make men moral, and what are the consequences of moral conduct. But it cannot get outside of the universe and lay down moral principles independent of all influences. I am well aware that in speaking of ethical questions upon this ground, I am exposed to many expressions of metaphysical contempt. I may hope to throw light upon the usual working of morality; but my theory of the facts cannot make men moral of itself. I cannot hope, for example, to show that immorality involves a contradiction, for I know that immorality exists. I cannot even hope to show that it is necessarily productive of misery to the individual, for I know that some people take pleasure in vicious conduct. I cannot deduce facts from morals, for I must consistently regard morals as part of the observed consequences of human nature under given conditions. Metaphysicians may, if they can, show me a more excellent method. I admit that their language sometimes enables them to take what, in words at least, is a sublimer position than mine. Kant's famous phrase, "Thou must, therefore thou canst," is impressive. And yet, it seems to me to involve an obvious piece of logical juggling. It is quite true that whenever it is my duty to act in a certain way, it must be a possibility; but that is only because an impossibility cannot be a duty. It is not my duty to fly, because I have not wings; and conversely, no doubt, it would follow that if it were my duty I must possess the organs required. Thus understood, however, the phrase loses its sublimity, and yet, it is only because we have so to understand it, that it has any plausibility. Admitting, however, that people who differ from me can use grander language, and confessing my readiness to admit error whenever they can point to a single fact attainable by the pure reason, I must keep to the humbler path. I speak of the moral instincts as of others, simply from the point of view of experience: I cannot myself discover a single truth from the abstract principle of non-contradiction; and am content to take for granted that the world exists as we know it to exist, without seeking to deduce its peculiarities by any high à priori road.

Upon this assumption, the question really resolves itself into a different one. We can neither explain nor justify the existence of pain; but, of course, we can ask whether, as a matter of fact, pain predominates over pleasure; and we can ask whether, as a matter of fact, the "cosmic processes" tend to promote or discourage virtuous conduct. Does the theory of the "struggle for existence" throw any new light upon the general problem? I am quite unable to see, for my own part, that it really makes any difference: evil exists; and the question whether evil predominates over good, can only, I should say, be decided by an appeal to experience. One source of evil is the conflict of interests. Every beast preys upon others; and man, according to the old saying, is a wolf to man. All that the Darwinian or any other theory can do is, to enable us to trace the consequences of this fact in certain directions; but it neither creates the fact nor makes it more or less an essential part of the process. It "explains" certain phenomena, in the sense of showing their connection with previous phenomena, but does not show why the phenomena should present themselves at all. If we indulge our minds in purely fanciful constructions, we may regard the actual system as good or bad, just as we choose to imagine for its alternative a better or a worse system. If everybody had been put into a world where there was no pain, or where each man could get all he wanted without interfering with his neighbours, we may fancy that things would have been pleasanter. If the struggle, which we all know to exist, had no effect in preventing the "survival of the fittest," things-so, at least, some of us may think-would have been worse. But such fancies have nothing to do with scientific inquiries. We have to take things as they are and make the best of them.

The common feeling, no doubt, is different. The incessant struggle between different races suggests a painful view of the universe, as Hobbes' natural state of war suggested painful theories as to human nature. War is evidently immoral, we think; and a doctrine which makes the whole process of evolution a process of war must be radically immoral too. The struggle, it is said, demands "ruthless self-assertion" and the hunting down of all competitors; and such phrases certainly have an unpleasant sound. But in the first place, the use of the epithets implies an anthropomorphism to which we have no right so long as we are dealing with the inferior species. We are then in a region to which such ideas have no direct application, and where the moral sentiments exist only in germ, if they can properly be said to exist at all. Is it fair to call a wolf ruthless because he eats a sheep and fails to consider the transaction from the sheep's point of view? We must surely admit that if the wolf is without mercy he is also without malice. We call an animal ferocious because a man who acted in the same way would be ferocious. But the man is really ferocious because he is really aware of the pain which he inflicts. The wolf, I suppose, has no more recognition of the sheep's feelings than a man has of feelings in the oyster or the potato. For him, they are simply non-existent; and it is just as inappropriate to think of the wolf as cruel, as it would be to call the sheep cruel for eating grass. Are we to say that "nature" is cruel because the arrangement increases the sum of undeserved suffering? That is a problem which I do not feel able to examine; but it is, at least, obvious that it cannot be answered off-hand in the affirmative. To the individual sheep it matters nothing whether he is eaten by the wolf or dies of disease or starvation. He has to die any way, and the particular way is unimportant. The wolf is simply one of the limiting forces upon sheep, and if he were removed others would come into play. The sheep, left to himself, would still give a practical illustration of the doctrine of Malthus. If, as evolutionists tell us, the hostility of the wolf tends to improve the breed of sheep, to encourage him to think more and to sharpen his wits, the sheep may be, on the whole, the better for the wolf, in this sense at least: that the sheep of a wolfless region might lead a more wretched existence, and be less capable animals and more subject to disease and starvation than the sheep in a wolf-haunted region. The wolf may, so far, be a blessing in disguise.

This suggests another obvious remark. When we speak of the struggle for existence, the popular view seems to construe this into the theory that the world is a mere cockpit, in which one race carries on an interminable struggle with the other. If the wolves are turned in with the sheep, the first result will be that all the sheep will become mutton, and the last that there will be one big wolf with all the others inside him. But this is contrary to the essence of the doctrine. Every race depends, we all hold, upon its environment, and the environment includes all the other races. If some, therefore, are in conflict, others are mutually necessary. If the wolf ate all the sheep, and the sheep ate all the grass, the result would be the extirpation of all the sheep and all the wolves, as well as all the grass. The struggle necessarily implies reciprocal dependence in a countless variety of ways. There is not only a conflict, but a system of tacit alliances. One species is necessary to the existence of others, though the multiplication of some implies also the dying out of particular rivals. The conflict implies no cruelty, as I have said, and the alliance no goodwill. The wolf neither loves the sheep (except as mutton) nor hates him; but he depends upon him as absolutely as if he were aware of the fact. The sheep is one of the wolf's necessaries of life. When we speak of the struggle for existence we mean, of course, that there is at any given period a certain equilibrium between all the existing species; it changes, though it changes so slowly that the process is imperceptible and difficult to realise even to the scientific imagination. The survival of any species involves the disappearance of rivals no more than the preservation of allies. The struggle, therefore, is so far from internecine that it necessarily involves co-operation. It cannot even be said that it necessarily implies suffering. People, indeed, speak as though the extinction of a race involved suffering in the same way as the slaughter of an individual. It is plain that this is not a necessary, though it may sometimes be the actual result. A corporation may be suppressed without injury to its members. Every individual will die before long, struggle or no struggle. If the rate of reproduction fails to keep up with the rate of extinction, the species must diminish. But this might happen without any increase of suffering. If the boys in a district discovered how to take birds' eggs, they might soon extirpate a species; but it does not follow that the birds would individually suffer. Perhaps they would feel themselves relieved from a disagreeable responsibility. The process by which a species is improved, the dying out of the least fit, implies no more suffering than we know to exist independently of any doctrine as to a struggle. When we use anthropomorphic language, we may speak of "self-assertion". But "self-assertion," minus the anthropomorphism, means self-preservation; and that is merely a way of describing the fact that an animal or plant which is well adapted to its conditions of life is more likely to live than an animal which is ill-adapted. I have some difficulty in imagining how any other arrangement can even be supposed possible. It seems to be almost an identical proposition that the healthiest and strongest will generally live longest; and the conception of a "struggle for existence" only enables us to understand how this results in certain progressive modifications of the species. If we could ever for a moment have fancied that there was no pain and disease, and that some beings were not more liable than others to those evils, I might admit that the new doctrine has made the world darker. As it is, it seems to me that it leaves the data just what they were before, and only shows us that they have certain previously unsuspected bearings upon the history of the world.

One other point must be mentioned. Not only are species interdependent as well as partly in competition, but there is an absolute dependence in all the higher species between its different members which may be said to imply a de facto altruism, as the dependence upon other species implies a de facto co-operation. Every animal, to say nothing else, is absolutely dependent for a considerable part of its existence upon its parents. The young bird or beast could not grow up unless its mother took care of it for a certain period. There is, therefore, no struggle as between mother and progeny; but, on the contrary, the closest possible alliance. Otherwise, life would be impossible. The young being defenceless, their parents could exterminate them if they pleased, and by so doing would exterminate the race. The parental relation, of course, constantly involves a partial sacrifice of the mother to her young. She has to go through a whole series of operations, which strain her own strength and endanger her own existence, but which are absolutely essential to the continuance of the race. It may be anthropomorphic to attribute any maternal emotions of the human kind to the animal. The bird, perhaps, sits upon her eggs because they give her an agreeable sensation, or, if you please, from a blind instinct which somehow determines her to the practice. She does not look forward, we may suppose, to bringing up a family, or speculate upon the delights of domestic affection. I only say that as a fact she behaves in a way which is at once injurious to her own chances of individual survival, and absolutely necessary to the survival of the species. The abnormal bird who deserts her nest escapes many dangers; but if all birds were devoid of the instinct, the birds would not survive a generation.

Now, I ask, what is the difference which takes place when the monkey gradually loses his tail and sets up a superior brain? Is it properly to be described as a development or improvement of the "cosmic process," or as the beginning of a prolonged contest against it?

In the first place, so far as man becomes a reasonable being, capable of foresight and of the adoption of means to ends, he recognises the nature of these tacit alliances. He believes it to be his interest not to exterminate everything, but to exterminate those species alone whose existence is incompatible with his own. The wolf eats every sheep that he comes across as long as his appetite lasts. If there are too many wolves, the process is checked by the starvation of the supernumerary eaters. Man can maintain just as many sheep as he wants, and may also proportion the numbers of his own species to the possibilities of future supply. Many of the lower species thus become subordinate parts of the social organism-that is to say, of the new equilibrium which has been established. There is so far a reciprocal advantage. The sheep that is preserved with a view to mutton gets the advantage, though he is not kept with a view to his own advantage. Of all arguments for vegetarianism, none is so weak as the argument from humanity. The pig has a stronger interest than any one in the demand for bacon. If all the world were Jewish, there would be no pigs at all. He has to pay for his privileges by an early death; but he makes a good bargain of it. He dies young, and, though we can hardly infer the "love of the gods," we must admit that he gets a superior race of beings to attend to his comforts, moved by the strongest possible interest in his health and vigour, and induced by its own needs, perhaps, to make him a little too fat for comfort, but certainly also to see that he has a good sty, and plenty to eat every day of his life. Other races, again, are extirpated as "ruthlessly" as in the merely instinctive struggle for existence. We get rid of wolves and snakes as well as we can, and more systematically than can be done by their animal competitors. The process does not necessarily involve cruelty, and certainly does not involve a diminution of the total of happiness. The struggle for existence means the substitution of a new system of equilibrium, in which one of the old discords has been removed, and the survivors live in greater harmony. If the wolf is extirpated as an internecine enemy, it is that there may be more sheep when sheep have become our allies and the objects of our earthly providence. The result may be, perhaps I might say must be, a state in which, on the whole, there is a greater amount of life supported on the planet; and therefore, as those will think who are not pessimists, a decided gain on the balance. At any rate, the difference so far is that the condition which was in all cases necessary, is now consciously recognised as necessary; and that we deliberately aim at a result which always had to be achieved on penalty of destruction. So far, again, as morality can be established on purely prudential grounds, the same holds good of relations between human beings themselves. Men begin to perceive that, even from a purely personal point of view, peace is preferable to war. If war is unhappily still prevalent, it is at least not war in which every clan is fighting with its neighbours, and where conquest means slavery or extirpation. Millions of men are at peace within the limits of a modern State, and can go about their business without cutting each other's throats. When they fight with other nations they do not enslave nor massacre their prisoners. Starting from the purely selfish ground Hobbes could prove conclusively that everybody benefited by the social compact which substituted peace and order for the original state of war. Is this, then, a reversal of the old state of things-a combating of a "cosmic process"? I should rather say that it is a development of the tacit alliances, and a modification so far of the direct or internecine conflict. Both were equally implied in the older conditions, and both still exist. Some races form alliances, while others are crowded out of existence. Of course, I cease to do some things which I should have done before. I don't attack the first man I meet in the street and take his scalp.

One reason is that I don't expect he will take mine; for, if I did, I fear that, even as a civilised being, I should try to anticipate his intentions. This merely means that we have both come to see that we have a common interest in keeping the peace. And this, again, merely means that the tacit alliance which was always an absolutely necessary condition of the survival of the species has now been extended through a wider area. The species could not have got on at all if there had not been so much alliance as is necessary for its reproduction and for the preservation of its young for some years of helplessness. The change is simply that the small circle which included only the primitive family or class has extended, so that we can meet members of the same nation, or, it may be, of the same race, on terms which were previously confined to the minor group. We have still to exterminate and still to preserve. The mode of employing our energies has changed, but not the essential nature. Morality proper, however, has so far not emerged. It begins when sympathy begins; when we really desire the happiness of others; or, as Kant says, when we treat other men as an end and not simply as a means. Undoubtedly this involves a new principle, no less than the essential principle of all true morality. Still, I have to ask whether it implies a combating or a continuation of a cosmic process. Now, as I have observed, even the animal mother shows what I have called a de facto altruism. She has instincts which, though dangerous to the individual, are essential for the race. The human mother sacrifices herself with a consciousness of the results to herself, and her personal fears are overcome by the strength of her affections. She intentionally endures a painful death to save them from suffering. The animal sacrifices herself, but without foresight of the result, and therefore without moral worth. This is merely the most striking exemplification of the general process of the development of morality. Conduct is first regarded purely with a view to the effects upon the agent, and is therefore enforced by extrinsic penalties, by consequences, that is, supposed to be attached to us by the will of some ruler, natural or supernatural. The instinct which comes to regard such conduct as bad in itself, which implies a dislike of giving pain to others, and not merely a dislike to the gallows, grows up under such probation until the really moralised being acquires feelings which make the external penalty superfluous. This, indubitably, is the greatest of all changes, the critical fact which decides whether we are to regard conduct simply as useful, or also to regard it as moral in the strictest sense. But I should still call it a development and not a reversal of the previous process. The conduct which we call virtuous is the same conduct externally which we before regarded as useful. The difference is that the simple fact of its utility, that is, of its utility to others and to the race in general, has now become also the sufficient motive for the action as well as the implicit cause of the action. In the earlier stages, when no true sympathy existed, men and animals were still forced to act in a certain way because it was beneficial to others. They now act in that way because they are conscious that it is beneficial to others. The whole history of moral evolution seems to imply this. We may go back to a period at which the moral law is identified with the general customs of the race; at which there is no perception of any clear distinction between that which is moral and that which is simply customary; between that which is imposed by a law in the strict sense and that which is dictated by general moral principles. In such a state of things, the motives for obedience partake of the nature of "blind instincts". No definite reason for them is present to the mind of the agent, and it does not occur to him even to demand a reason. "Our fathers did so and we do so" is the sole and sufficient explanation of their conduct. Thus instinct again may be traced back by evolutionists to the earliest period at which the instincts implied in the relations between the sexes or between parents and offspring, existed. They were the germ from which has sprung all morality such as we now recognise.

Morality, then, implies the development of certain instincts which are essential to the race, but which may, in an indefinite number of cases, be injurious to the individual. The particular mother is killed because she obeys her natural instincts; but, if it were not for mothers and their instincts, the race would come to an end. Professor Huxley speaks of the "fanatical individualism" of our time as failing to construct morality from the analogy of the cosmic process. An individualism which regards the cosmic process as equivalent simply to an internecine struggle of each against all, must certainly fail to construct a satisfactory morality upon such terms, and I will add that any individualism which fails to recognise fully the social character, which regards society as an aggregate instead of an organism, will, in my opinion, find itself in difficulties. But I also submit that the development of the instincts which directly correspond to the needs of the race, is merely another case in which we aim consciously at an end which was before an unintentional result of our actions. Every race, above the lowest, has instincts which are only intelligible by the requirements of the race; and has both to compete with some and to form alliances with others of its fellow occupants of the planet. Both in the unmoralised condition and in that in which morality has become most developed, these instincts have common characteristics, and may be regarded as conditions of the power of the race to which they belong to maintain its position in the world, and, speaking roughly, to preserve or increase its own vitality.

I will not pause to insist upon this so far as regards many qualities which are certainly moral, though they may be said to refer primarily to the individual. That chastity and temperance, truthfulness and energy, are, on the whole, advantages both to the individual and to the race, does not, I fancy, require elaborate proof; nor need I argue at length that the races in which they are common will therefore have inevitable advantages in the struggle for existence. Of all qualities which enable a race to hold its own, none is more important than the power of organising individually, politically, and socially, and that power implies the existence of justice and the instinct of mutual confidence-in short, all the social virtues. The difficulty seems to be felt in regard to those purely altruistic impulses, which, at first glance at any rate, make it apparently our duty to preserve those who would otherwise be unfit to live. Virtue, says Professor Huxley, is directed "not so much to the survival of the fittest," as to the "fitting of as many as possible to survive". I do not dispute the statement, I think it true in a sense; but I have a difficulty as to its application.

Morality, it is obvious, must be limited by the conditions in which we are placed. What is impossible is not a duty. One condition plainly is that the planet is limited. There is only room for a certain number of living beings; and though we may determine what shall be the number, we cannot arbitrarily say that it shall be indefinitely great. It is one consequence that we do, in fact, go on suppressing the unfit, and cannot help going on suppressing them. Is it desirable that it should be otherwise? Should we wish, for example, that America could still be a hunting-ground for savages? Is it better that it should contain a million red men or sixty millions of civilised whites? Undoubtedly the moralist will say with absolute truth that the methods of extirpation adopted by Spaniards and Englishmen were detestable. I need not say that I agree with him, and hope that such methods may be abolished wherever any remnant of them exists. But I say so partly because I believe in the struggle for existence. This process underlies morality, and operates whether we are moral or not. The most civilised race, that which has the greatest knowledge, skill, power of organisation, will, I hold, have an inevitable advantage in the struggle, even if it does not use the brutal means which are superfluous as well as cruel. All the natives who lived in America a hundred years ago would be dead now in any case, even if they had invariably been treated with the greatest humanity, fairness, and consideration. Had they been unable to suit themselves to new conditions of life, they would have suffered an euthanasia instead of a partial extirpation; and had they suited themselves they would either have been absorbed or become a useful part of the population. To abolish the old brutal method is not to abolish the struggle for existence, but to make the result depend upon a higher order of qualities than those of the mere piratical viking.

Mr. Pearson has been telling us in his most interesting book, that the negro may not improbably hold his own in Africa. I cannot say I regard this as an unmixed evil. Why should there not be parts of the world in which races of inferior intelligence or energy should hold their own? I am not so anxious to see the whole earth covered by an indefinite multiplication of the cockney type. But I only quote the suggestion for another reason. Till recent years the struggle for existence was carried on as between Europeans and negroes by simple violence and brutality. The slave trade and its consequences have condemned the whole continent to barbarism. That, undoubtedly, was part of the struggle for existence. But, if Mr. Pearson's guess should be verified, the results have been so far futile as well as disastrous. The negro has been degraded, and yet, after all our brutality, we cannot take his place. Therefore, besides the enormous evils to slave-trading countries themselves, the lowering of their moral tone, the substitution of piracy for legitimate commerce, and the degradation of the countries which bought the slaves, the superior race has not even been able to suppress the inferior. But the abolition of this monstrous evil does not involve the abolition but the humanisation of the struggle. The white man, however merciful he becomes, may gradually extend over such parts of the country as are suitable to him; and the black man will hold the rest and acquire such arts and civilisation as he is capable of appropriating. The absence of cruelty would not alter the fact that the fittest race would extend; but it may ensure that whatever is good in the negro may have a chance of development in his own sphere, and that success in the struggle will be decided by more valuable qualities.

Without venturing further into a rather speculative region, I need only indicate the bearing of such considerations upon problems nearer home. It is often complained that the tendency of modern civilisation is to preserve the weakly, and therefore to lower the vitality of the race. This seems to involve inadmissible assumptions. In the first place, the process by which the weaker are preserved consists in suppressing various conditions unfavourable to human life in general. Sanitary legislation, for example, aims at destroying the causes of many of the diseases from which our forefathers suffered. If we can suppress the smallpox, we of course save many weakly children, who would have died had they been attacked. But we also remove one of the causes which weakened the constitutions of many of the survivors. I do not know by what right we can say that such legislation, or again, the legislation which prevents the excessive labour of children, does more harm by preserving the weak than it does good by preventing the weakening of the strong. One thing is at any rate clear: to preserve life is to increase the population, and therefore to increase the competition; or, in other words, to intensify the struggle for existence. The process is as broad as it is long. If we could be sure that every child born should grow up to maturity, the result would be to double the severity of the competition for support, What we should have to show, therefore, in order to justify the inference of a deterioration due to this process, would be, not that it simply increased the number of the candidates for living, but that it gave to the feebler candidates a differential advantage; that they are now more fitted than they were before for ousting their superior neighbours from the chances of support. But I can see no reason for supposing such a consequence to be probable or even possible. The struggle for existence, as I have suggested, rests upon the unalterable facts that the world is limited and population elastic. Under all conceivable circumstances we shall still have in some way or other to proportion our numbers to our supplies; and under all circumstances those who are fittest by reason of intellectual or moral or physical qualities will have the best chance of occupying good places, and leaving descendants to supply the next generation. It is surely not less true that in the civilised as much as in the most barbarous race, the healthiest are the most likely to live, and the most likely to be ancestors. If so, the struggle will still be carried on upon the same principles, though certainly in a different shape.

It is true that this suggests one of the most difficult questions of the time. It is suggested, for example, that in some respects the "highest" specimens of the race are not the healthiest or the fittest. Genius, according to some people, is a variety of disease, and intellectual power is won by a diminution of reproductive power. A lower race, again, if we measure "high" and "low" by intellectual capacity, may oust a higher race, because it can support itself more cheaply, or, in other words, because it is more efficient for industrial purposes. Without presuming to pronounce upon such questions, I will simply ask whether this does not interpret Professor Huxley's remark about that "cosmic nature" which is still so strong, and which is likely to be strong so long as men require stomachs. We have not, I think, to suppress it, but to adapt it to new circumstances. We are engaged in working out a gigantic problem: What is the best, in the sense of the most efficient, type of human being? What is the best combination of brains and stomach? We turn out saints, who are "too good to live," and philosophers, who have run too rapidly to brains. They do not answer in practice, because they are instruments too delicate for the rough work of daily life. They may give us a foretaste of qualities which will be some day possible for the average man; of intellectual and moral qualities, which, though now exceptional, may become commonplace. But the best stock for the race are those in whom we have been lucky enough to strike out the happy combination, in which greater intellectual power is produced without the loss of physical vigour. Such men, it is probable, will not deviate so widely from the average type. The reconciliation of the two conditions can only be effected by a very gradual process of slowly edging onwards in the right direction. Meanwhile the theory of a struggle for existence justifies us, instead of condemning us, for preserving the delicate child, who may turn out to be a Newton or a Keats, because he will leave to us the advantage of his discoveries or his poems, while his physical feebleness assures us that he will not propagate his race.

This may lead to a final question. Does the morality of a race strengthen or weaken it; fit it to hold its own in the general equilibrium, or make its extirpation by low moral races more probable? I do not suppose that anybody would deny what I have already suggested, that the more moral the race, the more harmonious and the better organised, the better it is fitted for holding its own. But if this be admitted, we must also admit that the change is not that it has ceased to struggle, but that it struggles by different means. It holds its own, not merely by brute force, but by justice, humanity, and intelligence, while, it may be added, the possession of such qualities does not weaken the brute force, where such a quality is still required. The most civilised races are, of course, also the most formidable in war. But, if we take the opposite alternative, I must ask how any quality which really weakens the vitality of the race can properly be called moral. I should entirely repudiate any rule of conduct which could be shown to have such a tendency. This, indeed, indicates what seems to me to be the moral difficulty with most people. Charity, you say, is a virtue; charity increases beggary, and so far tends to produce a feebler population; therefore, a moral quality tends doubly to diminish the vigour of a nation. The answer is, of course, obvious, and I am confident that Professor Huxley would have so far agreed with me. It is that all charity which fosters a degraded class is therefore immoral. The "fanatical individualism" of to-day has its weaknesses; but in this matter it seems to me that we see the weakness of the not less fanatical "collectivism".

The question, in fact, how far any of the socialistic or ethical schemes of to-day are right or wrong, depends upon our answer to the question how far they tend to produce a vigorous or an enervated population. If I am asked to subscribe to General Booth's scheme, I inquire first whether the scheme is likely to increase or diminish the number of helpless hangers-on upon the efficient part of society. Will the whole nation consist in larger proportions of active and responsible workers, or of people who are simply burdens upon the real workers? The answer decides not only the question whether it is expedient, but also the question whether it is right or wrong, to support the proposed scheme. Every charitable action is so far a good action that it implies sympathy for suffering; but if it is so much in want of prudence that it increases the evil which it means to remedy, it becomes for that reason a bad action. To develop sympathy without developing foresight is just one of the one-sided developments which fail to constitute a real advance in morality, though I will not deny that it may incidentally lead to an advance.

I hold, then, that the "struggle for existence" belongs to an underlying order of facts to which moral epithets cannot be properly applied. It denotes a condition of which the moralist has to take account, and to which morality has to be adapted; but which, just because it is a "cosmic process," cannot be altered, however much we may alter the conduct which it dictates. Under all conceivable circumstances, the race has to adapt itself to the environment, and that necessarily implies a conflict as well as an alliance. The preservation of the fittest, which is surely a good thing, is merely another aspect of the dying out of the unfit, which is hardly a bad thing. The feast which Nature spreads before us, according to Malthus's metaphor, is only sufficient for a limited number of guests, and the one question is how to select them. The tendency of morality is to humanise the struggle, to minimise the suffering of those who lose the game; and to offer the prizes to the qualities which are advantageous to all, rather than to those which increase and intensify the bitterness of the conflict. This implies the growth of foresight, which is an extension of the earlier instinct, and enables men to adapt themselves to the future and to learn from the past, as well as to act up to immediate impulse of present events. It implies still more the development of the sympathy which makes every man feel for the hurts of all, and which, as social organisation is closer, and the dependence of each constituent atom upon the whole organisation is more vividly realised, extends the range of a man's interests beyond his own private needs. In that sense, again, it must stimulate "collectivism" at the expense of a crude individualism, and condemns the doctrine which, as Professor Huxley puts it, would forbid us to restrain the member of a community from doing his best to destroy it. To restrain such conduct is surely to carry on the conflict against all anti-social agents or tendencies. For I should certainly hold any form of collectivism to be immoral which denied the essential doctrine of the abused individualist, the necessity, that is, for individual responsibility. We have surely to suppress the murderer, as our ancestors suppressed the wolf. We have to suppress both the external enemies, the noxious animals whose existence is incompatible with our own, and the internal enemies which are injurious elements in the society itself. That is, we have to work for the same end of eliminating the least fit. Our methods are changed; we desire to suppress poverty, not to extirpate the poor man. We give inferior races a chance of taking whatever place they are fit for, and try to supplant them with the least possible severity if they are unfit for any place. But the suppression of poverty supposes not the confiscation of wealth, which would hardly suppress poverty in the long run, nor even the adoption of a system of living which would enable the idle and the good-for-nothing to survive. The progress of civilisation depends, I should say, on the extension of the sense of duty which each man owes to society at large. That involves such a constitution of society that, although we abandon the old methods of hanging and flogging and shooting down-methods which corrupted the inflicters of punishment by diminishing their own sense of responsibility-may give an advantage to the prudent and industrious, and make it more probable that they will be the ancestors of the next generation. A system which should equalise the advantages of the energetic and the helpless would begin by demoralising, and would very soon lead to an unprecedented intensification of the struggle for existence. The probable result of a ruthless socialism would be the adoption of very severe means for suppressing those who did not contribute their share of work. But, in any case, as it seems, we never get away or break away from the inevitable fact. If individual ends could be suppressed, if every man worked for the good of society as energetically as for his own, we should still feel the absolute necessity of proportioning the whole body to the whole supplies obtainable from the planet, and to preserve the equilibrium of mankind relatively to the rest of nature. That day is probably distant; but even upon that hypothesis the struggle for existence would still be with us, and there would be the same necessity for preserving the fittest and killing out, as gently as might be, those who were unfit.